PENTECOST 3

Interpreting the Lessons of the Church Year

William Klassen

PENTECOST 3

PROCLAMATION 6 | SERIES A

FORTRESS PRESS | MINNEAPOLIS

PROCLAMATION 6
Interpreting the Lessons of the Church Year
Series A, Pentecost 3

Scripture quotations, unless otherwise noted or translated from the Greek by the author, are from the New Revised Standard Version Bible, copyright © 1989 by the Division of Christian Education of the National Council of Churches in the U.S.A. and used by permission.

The lectionary readings in this volume are arranged specifically for use in 1996. The coordination of propers, Sundays in Ordinary Time, and Sundays after Pentecost may vary in other years where cycle A is used.

Cover design: Ellen Maly
Text design: David Lott

The Library of Congress has cataloged the first four volumes as follows:

Proclamation 6, Series A : interpreting the lessons of the church
    year.
        p.   cm.
    Contents: [1] Advent/Christmas / J. Christian Beker — [2]
Epiphany / Susan K. Hedahl — [3] Lent / Peter J. Gomes —[4] Holy
Week / Robin Scroggs.
        ISBN 0-8006-4207-4 (v. 1 : alk. paper) — ISBN 0-8006-4208-2 (v.
2 : alk. paper) — ISBN 0-8006-4209-0 (v. 3 : alk. paper) — ISBN 0-8006-4210-4
(v. 4 : alk. paper).
        1. Bible—Homiletical use. 2. Bible—liturgical lessons,
English.
    BS534.5P74 1995
    251—dc20   95-4622
                                                                    CIP

            Easter / Gordon Lathrop—ISBN 0-8006-4211-2 (v. 5: alk. paper)
            Pentecost 1 / K. C. Hanson—ISBN 0-8006-4212-0 (v. 6: alk. paper)
            Pentecost 2 / Clarice J. Martin—ISBN 0-8006-4213-9 (v. 7: alk. paper)
            Pentecost 3 / William Klassen—ISBN 0-8006-4214-7 (v. 8: alk. paper)

The paper used in this publication meets the minimum requirements of American National Standard for Information Sciences—Permanence of Paper for Printed Library Materials, ANSI Z329.48-1948.

Manufactured in the U.S.A.   AF 1-4214
00   99   98   97   96   1   2   3   4   5   6   7   8   9   10

Contents

Introduction

WHAT WE ARE ABOUT

This book seeks to stimulate discussion about the Bible, written at least two thousand years ago, and its relevance for modern living. It is directed at persons who are commissioned by the church to work with people untrained in the Bible. The messenger is the human medium through which the gap is overcome between materials written long ago and the current scene, the one called and trained to proclaim the word of God at least on Sunday morning but also on other occasions.

To focus our assignment even more, however, we follow the ancient Christian custom of using a lectionary. Ancient lectionaries were created because few Bibles were available. Today many denominations consider it good to follow lectionary selections previously agreed on. Thus Christians in many places and many confessions study the same text on a Sunday morning. We affirm in this way our oneness of faith in Christ.

The modern lectionary also goes beyond ancient ones in combining readings from the prophets, the Psalms, the epistles, and the Gospels. Great care has been taken to bring together biblical themes from the various Scripture selections.

As the spiritual leader of your flock, you will want to tailor all of this material to your own peculiar needs. What is offered here are starters: one believer's reaction to what he has lived, read, and experienced. These studies represent results from a lifetime of Bible study and teaching, half of it based in a university, the other half in a seminary, but always nurtured to an unusual degree in a local congregation. My reception by the church has always been treasured as a special gift and my joy in preaching has grown from year to year. Somehow a text has never achieved its fullest degree of understanding until I have lived it and have preached it to God's people. I owe a special debt to the good people of the Toronto United Mennonite Church who elected me to serve on their preaching team for a number of years. Preaching, I believe, is a team effort. In Toronto I learned how joyful and rewarding it could be.

THE SEASON OF PENTECOST

During this season of the church year, special opportunities are offered to relate the redeeming action of God to our world. Such issues as ecological responsibility, interfaith dialogue, or peace, slander, and our relationship to the stranger, all invite us to listen to previous people of God through the lectionary readings.

Once I was asked to cover for a minister on Peace Sunday. In his kind invitation, he specified that there was no need to devote a whole sermon to peace, but perhaps I could pay some attention to it in my message and in my prayers. So much for a central biblical theme and an urgent need for our world today! For, more than perhaps anything else, our century is one of war. The relation of God's people to war continues to be an urgent issue.

As I discovered then, lectionary selections have not been as conscious as they should be of the place that peace has in the Bible. Think of the enormous strides forward in virtually all denominations in the development of a theology of peace. One grieves the continuing loss of lives through war in many places, and especially one fears the ways in which religions are inevitably drawn into ethnic conflicts and into such dubious, if not demonic, ventures as "ethnic cleansing." Even Christians in the Middle East think they can achieve something by fighting against their Jewish or Muslim neighbors. Other Christian brothers, such as Elias Chacour, Naim Ateek, and Jonathan Kuttab, as well as Christian sisters, such as Jean Zaru and Hanan Ashrawi, are just a few of the strong leaders finding a way beyond violence toward peace .

The Roman Catholic Church has for some years now encouraged the practice of a prayer for peace in each service. We can all do with such. Above all, it is time that we celebrate the peace achieved in South Africa, the peace process being achieved in the Middle East, and that which is emerging in Ireland. Let no one minimize the role Christians have played and continue to play in these achievements.

Hillel, the contemporary of Jesus, once said, "Be of the disciples of Aaron, one that loves peace, that loves humankind, and brings them near to Torah." A descendent of his declared that the world rests upon three things: on truth, on judgment, and on peace (see Zech. 8:16, 18, and 19, where God is described as one who sows peace). Israel is urged to be courageous, and to love truth and peace.

A LOCAL EXAMPLE

The congregation of which I am a part has, for the past two years, worked with a Jewish congregation to see whether we could jointly build a place of worship and study. So far we are able to proceed, and by the time you read this, we should be in our new building.

That experience has been a transforming one for our emerging congregation. There is an excitement among us we missed when we thought in more conventional terms. There is, moreover, a vitality that has come to us as we have studied our roots in Judaism and tried to understand why certain things we took for granted were not acceptable to our faith partners. In short, we have been able to sense something of the passion of Micah, Ezekiel, and Isaiah, seen the joy of wisdom and of the Law, and witnessed the excitement Matthew's community had as it built for the future. In their establishment of boundary limits, however, Matthew's community was hampered by a perception of Jewish unfaithfulness that does not plague us.

Consider introducing your congregation to the richness of our mother/sister faith, Judaism. Consider inviting a Jew to come to your people and explain their faith. The rich collection of readings from the Jewish prophets have nurtured Christians for many centuries. Although they were born in Jewish communities and their indictments were forged many years ago, the prophets speak to us today because our problems are so similar.

PEACE AND LOVE INSIDE THE CHURCH

Peace is threatened most severely within the church itself. In part that is so because we have not applied theories of conflict resolution to the church's internal life, settling at times for conflict management instead. Nothing could be further from the power of the gospel, since it is reconciliation, not the management of conflict, that the gospel offers to us.

Beyond the borders of our own congregations the fight really gets going when we debate whether sexual orientation can be used to exclude persons from the church or its ministry. All of this represents, from the perspective of our lectionary readings, a compelling invitation to dialogue, and an invitation to share with each other what the Holy Spirit is saying to the church today.

We need desperately a forum in which these issues can be debated in Christian love. Our sermons can be a stimulant for such dialogue. For an excellent example of peacemaking in the church, with a healthy dose of humor, read Garrison Keillor's story "Brethren" in his collection, *Leaving Home* (New York; Viking, 1987). As we look again at the commandment to "love your neighbor," let us remember that it applies first to our families and then to the local parish in which we live and work.

AN INVITATION TO DIALOGUE

Markus Barth once described the writings of the Bible as dialogues between God and the author. The biblical text before us is to be seen, he suggests, not so much as God's word to us as it is the reply that the writers give in their dialogue with God. We are eavesdropping on that conversation when we read the Bible. Amazingly, as we get caught up in the conversation, we discover that they are talking about us, like a hospital patient overhearing a doctor and a nurse speaking about the patient's condition, saying, "Yes, the patient was mortally ill, but will rally and recover." Or it is as if a lawyer and judge are huddling and we hear them say, "The accused is guilty but will be acquitted."

Similarly, as you prepare your sermons from Sunday to Sunday, think of your task as being to draw your people into eavesdropping on some important dialogues going on in the past which could, in turn, stimulate reflection and dialogue among your people. Søren Kierkegaard thought of the Bible as a love letter—God's love letter. What an intriguing assignment to work from week to week as the one who tries to interpret that love letter! Our assignment, then, is not only to try to interpret every phrase exactly and locate the strata from which it comes but ultimately to help people see that they are precisely the persons whom God loves strongly and without end.

At numerous places in the Bible writers use expressions such as "I write this that our joy may be complete." Paul describes his ministry as being a "co-worker for your joy." Since time immemorial Jews and Christians have distinguished themselves among their contemporaries by their joy. There is no reason that cannot happen in your community through the weeks ahead. "Let them sing better songs before I believe in their savior," Nietzsche grumbled. He had a point.

BOOK NOTES

Since at least two of the readings used in this season come from prison (Philippians, 2 Timothy) and address the themes of suffering and forgiveness from that context, attention should be drawn to a considerable literature produced under adverse conditions in our time. As one example, note the superb books that have been written by people held hostage in Lebanon, such as Terry Anderson, Benjamin Weir, and Terry Waite. Especially appropriate to consider while studying these lessons is Lawrence Jenko's *Bound to Forgive* (Notre Dame, Ind.: Ave Maria Press, 1995). These books are moving testimonials on what years of confinement as hostages can do to spiritual growth.

Eighteenth Sunday after Pentecost
Twenty-Fifth Sunday in Ordinary Time
Proper 21

Lectionary	First Lesson	Psalm	Second Lesson	Gospel
Revised Common	Ezek. 18:1-4, 25-32	Ps. 25:1-9	Phil. 2:1-13	Matt. 21:23-32
Episcopal (BCP)	Ezek. 18:1-4, 25-32	Psalm 25:1-14 or 25:3-9	Phil. 2:1-13	Matt. 21:28-32
Roman Catholic	Isa. 55:6-9	Ps. 145:2-3, 8-9, 17-18	Phil. 1:20c-24, 27a	Matt. 20:1-16
Lutheran (LBW)	Isa. 55:6-9	Ps. 27:1-13	Phil. 1:1-5(6-11), 19-27	Matt. 20:1-16

HERMENEUTICAL REFLECTIONS

The common thread that runs throughout these readings from both the Hebrew Bible and the writings of the new community in Christ is the reminder to the addressees that the justice of God needs to be respected. The early Christians typically saw forgiveness as an integral aspect of the *justice* of God—"If we confess our sins, He is faithful and just and will forgive us our sins" (1 John 1:9; 2:1). Here the forgiveness of God is rooted in God's fundamental justice and faithfulness; it never rests on God's love or mercy. Neither is pity the essential element or the basis of the appeal (as in Isaiah 55:7).

Some years ago, the leader of the Soviet Union, Mikhail Gorbachev, through policies of *glasnost* and *perestroika*, led his country in a collective act of repentance. He stepped down and made room for a new political reality to emerge. At about the same time, a film by Tengiz Abuladze called *Repentance* was very popular throughout the country.

Repentance is a mark of strength; it is an admission that we need to change course and are prepared to do so. Repentance is the secret to renewal and the only hope for growth, whether in one's personal life or in the life of the church or the nation. Think only of what has happened in South Africa in the last ten years, or in Ireland and the Middle East. In South Africa, Nelson Mandela has shown enormous strength in his ability to forgive those who did him great harm by imprisoning him for thirty years, refusing to seek revenge on his oppressors. He has learned to place his country's needs first, giving precedence to the people whom he serves.

FIRST LESSON: ISAIAH 55:6-9

An early statement about God's nature as love is found in the book of Hosea. Noteworthy is the affirmation that God's love is above human love.

PENTECOST 3—SERIES A

The ways of God are not human ways, the thoughts of God are not human thoughts. This text from Second Isaiah written at the end of the exile, long after the exodus and Hosea, even two centuries after First Isaiah when the people of Israel had gone through even more trials and tribulations and more periods of unfaithfulness, is a call of return to seek the Lord and to call upon God. It is an invitation to accept the pardon, the mercy, and the forgiveness of God.

The clearest statement in Hebrew literature, profoundly defining God as a forgiving God, is Exodus 34:6-7. There, at the very time that the covenant was being made and Moses was on Mount Sinai, the people were unfaithful to that covenant. At the same time, God's nature is defined as "merciful and gracious, slow to anger . . . forgiving iniquity and transgression and sin."

This fundamental definition of God is what Isaiah invites his people to experience in a renewed way. "Turn back to Yahweh, who will pity, to our God who is rich in forgiving" (55:7). Whatever God is for the Israelites, there is no room for a view of God that makes the Divine simply an expression of the human. The otherness of God, the transcendence of God, is very deeply affirmed in this classic passage attributed to Isaiah from the sixth or fifth century.

The words from Ezekiel 18 (treated next week) revolve around the same issue. The form of address is that of the law court. Can God be considered just? Is God fair? Ezekiel affirms the fairness of God because God continues to invite people to repent. Those who do repent, that is, who change their ways, can count on being saved. No longer will the children have to suffer for their parents' sin. Each one will bear responsibility for their own actions. God has no pleasure in the death of anyone and, therefore, invites everyone to repent and to return toward life. God, the Creator of Life, delights in the fullness of life for all created things. God confronts the people and commands them to listen. They are invited to face their own injustice, to shake off their sins committed against God, and to repent. A new heart and a new spirit is available which will avoid all occasions of sin. Repentance leads to life, God's wish for them.

(For Ezek. 18:1-4, 25-32, see the Nineteenth Sunday after Pentecost.)

SECOND LESSON: PHILIPPIANS 1:20-24, 27

Philippians is one of the finest tributes to the strength of the Christian faith, as described by the apostle Paul. Although in prison, he rejoices that other people are preaching the gospel and that, precisely because Paul is out of the way, they seem to have more freedom to do so. At the same time, he nurtures his ties with the Philippians and expresses his joy at the solidarity of their prayers for him and the support that he has received from them. He then expresses the passionate hope that he will have no cause for shame but shall be able to "speak boldly" through his whole life, whether he dies or lives.

The characteristically Christian term *boldness* is one also used widely by the Cynics of Paul's day. For them it meant they could speak anything wherever they wanted to and carry out whatever act, whether in private or in public, they felt led to carry out. It was the hallmark of their existence.

Boldness is also a basic defining term in the New Testament. The early Christian community, however, saw in it an opportunity to speak forthrightly for a redemptive purpose, as shown in Jesus' words about his impending death (Mark 8:32), or in the disciples' conversations with each other (2 Cor. 7:4). The disciples also spoke to God in this way, borrowing from the experience of Job (23:3-4), and with one another.

Each of these New Testament writers (Luke, Hebrews, Paul, John) uses the term in his own particular way; for Paul it has to do with the proclamation of the gospel and the building of the community. There is no timidity or fear, only courage to speak of one's experiences with Christ.

That affirmation reverberates with the clarity of a trumpet here in verse 21. The essence of Paul's life, he says, is defined by his relation to Christ. When that is the case, death is a gain. This is not a Socratic praise of death, whether noble or ignoble, but rather a profoundly Christian affirmation that since one is united with Christ, it is immaterial whether one is in this world or in the next.

At the same time, Paul raises the question whether his own life here continues to have a purpose. If so, then he is hard put what to choose. He cannot really tell whether he wants to live or die. On the one hand, he has a certain eager desire (the Greek word means an uncontrollable desire, often translated "lust") to depart to be with Christ, which is better by far. At the same time, for the sake of the Philippians, there is greater need for him to stay in the body.

In the meantime, his predominant wish is that if he stays, he wants to see for himself how the Philippians are "standing firm, one in spirit, one in mind, contesting or contending as one for the gospel of faith encountering one's opponents with not so much as a tremor" (Phil. 1:27-28). With this military metaphor, Paul denotes the key goal he has set. It is the oneness in spirit and oneness in mind, which is the essence of the church. For this he strives and for this he works. He invites the Philippians to join him in this struggle.

Soldiers of Christ. The Jerusalem Bible titles the section on Philippians 1:27-30 "Fight for the Faith." The appeals to "stand firm," to "[strive] side by side," to be "unshaken by your enemies," and the language of victory and struggle, indicate that for Paul the military imagery of a battle is of some importance. A later writer, seeking to do justice to Paul, developed brilliantly the imagery of the Christian armor in even greater detail (Eph. 6:10-20).

The church today has little use for this imagery. Our hymn books are increasingly expunged of all military imagery, and hymns like "Onward Christian Soldiers" or even "A Mighty Fortress" will hardly survive in the mainline Christian denominations.

Already in its first three hundred years, the church flirted with military metaphors; one of the titles some Christians chose for themselves was "soldiers of Christ." This emphasized those aspects of the Christian life that are integral to soldiering: solidarity and unity, combining efforts and working together, and overcoming fear. It lacked, however, the warmth of the image of the church as a family and of Christians as friends. Moreover, the highly structured organization of the army, superiors and inferiors, all were in fundamental conflict with the Christian communities of love and their goal to foster life. Both sought to make peace, but their methods were quite different.

The military metaphor reminds us, however, that fundamentally life is a struggle. We engage in battle not against flesh and blood but against unseen powers that are hard to name. Our Muslim friends speak of a *jihad,* meaning the spiritual struggle that is waged in the hearts and minds of us all—the battle between good and evil. Paul is convinced that the Philippians will win. Their salvation will come from God, however, but the victory will be theirs.

Paul argues in Romans 16:17-20 along a similar line. There he urges his readers to avoid those who create dissensions among them, to remain obedient, and to remain wise in what is good and simple with respect to evil. Then "the God of peace will shortly crush Satan under your feet" (16:20). God crushes the evil, but under their feet! Moreover, it is the God of peace—not the God of war—who wins the battle, but that can only happen when the community affirms its solidarity and its oneness. This rich collection of metaphors, going back to centuries before the time of Jesus, later became a major source of inspiration to many Christians—both those who avoided war (Benedictines) and those who did not (Salvation Army). Can the church do away with all these military metaphors and still survive?

The irony is that nothing unites people like a war. One can only hope that Christians can be united without a literal war. Perhaps Paul reminds us that life is a struggle and if Jesus could not avoid a battle with evil, neither can we.

(For Phil. 2:1-13, see the Nineteenth Sunday after Pentecost.)

GOSPEL: MATTHEW 20:1-16

The finest commentary on this Parable of the Workers in the Vineyard is by Luise Schottroff (in the book *God of the Lowly* [ed. Willie Schottroff and Wolfgang Stegemann (Maryknoll, N.Y.: Orbis, 1988)], 129–47). A brief summary may be useful since it offers us a new perspective on this story.

Schottroff urges us to treat the parable as a real-life story and not as an allegory. It is essential therefore that we try to learn as much detail from it as possible and that we see it in its social context. The parable presupposes that employers would get this kind of help for as little outlay as possible. In addition to an agreed wage, which was usually haggled, the employer had to feed the day laborer too.

Schottroff finds the parable plausible in all its details; only the generosity of the owner is unusual. In the context of Matthew, it is clearly meant to stress the point that the last shall be first and the first shall be last (19:14, 30; 20:20-28). The owner agrees to pay the first laborers the usual wage for one day's work, one denarius. To later recruits, he says, "whatever is right I will give you." Since the harvest was ready, there could be no delay and since the recruitment at dawn was not adequate, the owner recruits all day long, at nine o'clock, at noon, at three o'clock, and at five o'clock. The men whom he invited at eventide were unemployed, as is clear from their plaintive words: "No one has hired us" (v. 7). These day laborers had no rights. They were happy to get any work they could and, above all, during harvest they had no bargaining power.

Two crucial points emerge: The parable intends to speak first of the goodness or generosity of God (see v. 15) and, second, of the behavior of human beings toward one another in contrast with God's behavior. Note, for example, the envy and grumbling of those who worked the longer shift.

The parable is not intended as social criticism, but to tell of the goodness of God. Schottroff observes that it is not concerned about recompense but rather with the use of the sense of justice as a weapon against other human beings. Solidarity should exist among the workers in the vineyard, but the long shift workers say, "You have made them equal to us." Matthew uses the parable to cope with a painful and pernicious conflict in his community, not to explain general or even supratemporal theological ideas.

Matthew 20:1-28 deals with the question, Who is "first among you?" For Matthew, this story means that there are Christians who claim privileges in God's service because, in fact, they do more than the "little ones" in the community. Their claim to privileges before God and, therefore, in the community as well offends against solidarity—"You are all brothers." Schottroff thinks the parable is early and shows the same gentle courting of the Pharisees found in the earliest Jesus tradition.

This parable relates to the questions posed by both Isaiah and Ezekiel whether God is faithful even when acting in unpredictable and unforeseen ways. It was Jewish custom in Jesus' day that everyone was paid a daily wage regardless of how many hours he or she worked. So, in a way, those who considered the master unfair and complained that everyone was paid the same were told that the master was simply abiding by custom. Certainly, the owner is "free to do what I like with my own money" (v. 15). Why should anyone begrudge the other when, eventually, the last will be first and the first last? The contract was honored for all.

In an essential way, this parable points to the heart of the gospel, which is a great equalizer. We are not paid according to our merits, but according to the generous nature of God, who applies only one criterion, the standard of mercy.

(For Matt. 21:28-32, see the Nineteenth Sunday after Pentecost.)

HOMILETICAL REFLECTIONS

Paul provides us with a glimpse into his life's priorities when he says he has only one hope and one eager expectation that Christ may be made large in his body. This beautiful biblical word "to be magnified" ("be honored," "be glorified") is well known from Mary's song in Luke, where she prays that her soul may magnify the Lord (1:46). The Westminster catechism has it that the chief end of humans is to "glorify God and to enjoy God" forever. Can we get behind the cliché? Karl Barth puts it well: "If our souls magnify anyone, then certainly not the Lord but ourselves!" And while God has no need to be magnified by us, God still wants to be extolled within our wretched life. That extolling, Barth maintains, consists simply in this: That at every step we let God be Lord in our thoughts, our conscience, and our inner life and let God bring forth wholeness in the midst of the unwholeness of our existence.

Visualize Paul as he sits in prison and reviews his life. We preachers can understand, for we are out in front of people, "under review" at all times. We are then tempted, often ever so subtly, to put in a good word for ourselves. After all, how can we effectively lead the people unless they think well of us?

But Paul begins with a thoroughly biblical perspective, which is to let God be at the center of the stage (see Acts 10:46; 19:17). As a preacher, he is a coach spurring the team on. The preacher is never the actor seeking to be magnified. We are stagehands, that is all. Our task is to let the greatness of God become magnified. The words attributed to John the Baptist about his relation to Jesus apply as well to us: "He must grow greater, I must grow smaller" (John 3:30). In our narcissistic age where we are deeply saturated with the cult of self-advancement, this invitation to magnify Christ is often muted and we lose sight of our goal.

Paul reminds us that true joy, a strong sense of mission, and the courage to affirm the greatness of God's forgiving power can only come when our chief goal is the advancement of God, not our own advancement. Joy is the "most rare, the most scarce commodity in the world" (Karl Barth) because we seek the lesser goals.

One of the reasons that the Hebrew faith (including, of course, Isaiah and Ezekiel) has such a great celebration of joy, found in Jesus and Paul as well, is that they focus not on their own personal happiness, but on the covenant that they have with Yahweh. Joy comes from being joined at all levels with the Creator's purposes in life. Then the God of Life becomes great in the lives of others and we achieve our goal in life that God (love, peace, joy) would become a stronger presence, a more dominant force in peoples' lives.

Nineteenth Sunday after Pentecost
Twenty-Sixth Sunday in Ordinary Time
Proper 22

Lectionary	First Lesson	Psalm	Second Lesson	Gospel
Revised Common	Isa. 5:1-7	Ps. 80:7-15	Phil. 3:4b-14	Matt. 21:33-46
Episcopal (BCP)	Isa. 5:1-7	Psalm 80 or 80:7-14	Phil. 3:14-21	Matt. 21:33-43
Roman Catholic	Ezek. 18:25-28	Ps. 25:2-9	Phil. 2:1-11 or 2:1-5	Matt. 21:28-32
Lutheran (LBW)	Ezek. 18:1-4, 25-32	Ps. 25:1-9	Phil. 2:1-5(6-11)	Matt. 21:28-32

FIRST LESSON: EZEKIEL 18:1-4, 25-28

Ezekiel is often called the prophet of individual responsibility. The affirmation that summarizes his position most clearly is "It is the son that sins, and no other, that shall die: a son shall not share a father's guilt nor a father his son's. The wicked man reaps the fruit of his own wickedness, the righteous reap the fruit of their own righteousness" (Ezek. 18:19-20).

There is apparently a strong note of contention between the people and God on this issue. It comes to its climax, perhaps, in the words "Listen, you Israelites, it is you who act without principle, and not I." Obviously, a debate is being carried on about who is acting without paying any attention to justice.

In that controversy, God makes one simple statement, and it is repeated often by the prophet. It is the inexorable law of plant life, known to every gardener and farmer, that when you sow wheat, you reap wheat; when you sow weeds, you reap weeds. At the same time, allowance is made for "a wicked person turning from wicked ways, perceiving what is just and what is right, and by turning, is saved." Life comes from seeing yourself as you are, especially seeing your offenses as they are, and turning your back on them. Ezekiel, as did all the prophets, had at the center of his message the offer for repentance.

This is why the story of Jonah is such a comedy of errors. Jonah thinks he can be a prophet without preaching repentance. Even when he is forced to do so, he thinks he can still maintain his status as a prophet even though he rejects the repentance of the people of Nineveh. But the author makes it clear, in a very humorous way, that Jonah has it all wrong. The Hebrew word *shuv,* "turn about," as well as the Greek word for repentance, *metanoia,* are strongly rooted in the will, and both refer to a changed mind that leads to a different kind of behavior.

As always, when the Bible talks about human action, emotions and rationality are joined together. While the emphasis rests on rationality, most important is the resulting action—not what you say but what you do. The texts from the Gospel this week beautifully illustrate this. We tend, of course, to shade these terms and rub out the sharp distinctions between the categories of righteous and evil. At the same time, the terms that are used here, justice and evil, or righteousness and unrighteousness, are fundamental to the way our society operates even today. No one affirmed more strongly the individual moral responsibility of each person than Ezekiel.

(For Isa. 5:1-7, see the Twentieth Sunday after Pentecost.)

SECOND LESSON: PHILIPPIANS 2:1-11

Like Ezekiel, Paul is concerned about the way the community lives and he calls the community to do away with rivalry and personal vanity. Instead, he invites them humbly to reckon others "better than yourselves." He urges them to look to each other's interests and not merely to their own. This fervent passion for thinking alike and feeling alike as the way love expresses itself in the community Paul seeks most urgently for the Philippians.

To have "one mind" and to have a care and commitment to community, to oneness, is basic to being a church. In Philippi, as well as in Corinth and other places, this was not an easy goal to achieve. It is, of course, no different in many other periods of the history or in other places of the church. Many varied definitions of the church exist, but few follow Paul in defining a church by unanimity.

One British author says Paul uses a theological sledgehammer to crack an ethical nut when he brings the full weight of the incarnation to bear upon this issue. That is, he urges his readers to behave toward one another as they have learned from Christ. Jesus, being in the form of God, sharing in the divine nature, left the state of equality with God and made himself nothing. How drastically the incarnation is here defined and how acutely it is applied to common, ordinary problems! Jesus became a slave. He revealed himself in human shape, took on human likeness, humbled himself, and accepted death, even death on a cross.

The most shameful death known to the ancient world was taken on by the Son of God himself providing a model par excellence for the Christian life. Note, however, that whenever the New Testament upholds the model of following Jesus or imitating Jesus, it never selects his celibacy, his beard, or his sandals, but always goes to the heart of what is known as *kenosis,* that is, the emptying of himself and becoming like us in every respect.

Because of this, God raised him to the heights, and he deserves now the name above all names. Paul affirms his belief—as did the early church—that at the name of Jesus every knee in heaven, on earth, and in the depths bows. The goal of human history is that every tongue may confess that Jesus Christ is Lord to the glory of God the Father. In faithfulness to the model Jesus has provided, it will be achieved through gentle persuasion.

The lordship of Christ is again a metaphor that needs to be translated into our own idiom. It is a problematic metaphor, as the World Council of Churches discovered some time ago when they proposed it as a theme and found that Third World Christians had trouble with its connotations of overlording. The theme that replaced it, "Christ the Light of the World," made the same basic affirmation without the connotations of colonialism. Most of us do not generally acknowledge that we have lords. We are independent, self-sufficient, and answer to no one but our own conscience. That, of course, is not the way Paul views human life; certainly not life in Christ.

It should be observed, however, that Paul puts together two very important aspects of the Christian life, "You must work out your own salvation" (v. 12), but also, "It is God that works in you, inspiring both the will and the deed for God's own chosen purpose" (v. 13). Fundamentally, Paul tells the Philippians, "you are on your own." He is absent from them, but they still have the resource of God to rely upon and, in fact, become co-workers with God in working out their own salvation. This, to be sure, is also done in fear and in trembling. Again, individual responsibility, as in Ezekiel, is urgently asserted here. The strongest affirmation of the self is thus retained.

We are here at the heart of Christology—the convictions Christians hold about Jesus as Messiah. Jews brought into human history the idea of the Messiah and there are disagreements about the utility of this idea. Aberrations undoubtedly abound and a "messianic" complex has entered the diagnostic manuals of psychiatry; occasionally one meets such severely disoriented people. The Messiah was, for Judaism, always a symbol of hope.

Christians differ from Jews in one fundamental affirmation: "The hopes and fears of all the years are met in thee tonight," we sing at Christmas, and thus affirm that we no longer look for a Messiah. Rather, we are members of a messianic community who see in Jesus the bodily fullness of the Godhead. It is hard enough to unpack such an affirmation of faith, but even harder to go one step further and accept our mission as members of the body of Christ today. What is important here is not the definitions, philosophical or psychological. Above all, the most important agenda is not to convince each other that this or that definition is right. Rather, we are to act as one. As Jesus put it, according to John, in his final will and testament, his prayer for us: "That they may be one . . . so that the world may know" (John 17:11, 21). Jesus never prayed for the unity of the church, but he probably did pray that the church might be one, even as God and he are one. Paul appreciated the importance of that prayer.

(For Phil. 3:14-21, see the Twentieth Sunday after Pentecost.)

GOSPEL: MATTHEW 21:28-32

This Parable of the Two Sons is the first of three parables of judgment. Matthew is the only one to present this parable. The second parable of the three comes from Mark and the third from Q, the common source for Luke and Matthew. It plays a transitional role, picking up that which has gone before and pointing forward to that which is to come. It is also related closely to the preceding dispute with the chief priests and the elders. The point of the parable is to emphasize the guilt of the son who is disobedient, even though he claims he will do what his father asks. The distinction between the two sons is not between Jew and Gentile, but between two kinds of behavior, what Ben Viviano calls the "faithless leaders and faithful outcasts," the true and the false Israel.

The fundamental test in the New Testament, moreover, is always whether the will of the Father, the will of God, is being done. The summary of this section, in which Jesus says that the tax gatherers and prostitutes are pressing ahead into the kingdom ahead of the others, is an application of the parable to the situation that gave it birth.

High praise is given to John the Baptist who "showed you the right way to live" (21:32). All of the teachings of the kingdom, found in Matthew, can be summarized in this phrase, the way of justice. It is in close harmony also with what Ezekiel taught.

In this very pithy and short story, Jesus helps them to think through the issues: "What do you think?" (v. 28). His appeal is always to their thinking. In this particular case, he demonstrates the human tendency to snap to attention and say "Yes, sir!" when we are asked to do something by our Lord. At the same time, it is quite a different story to actually go ahead and live the way of righteousness.

The key to the narrative, as in Ezekiel, is the word *repentance,* which does not appear literally in this text. The word used in v. 29 to describe the way in which the son had changed his mind and in v. 32 to describe the call for the priests and elders to change their minds, has to do with primarily a change of course or direction. It is the word also used to describe

Judas's change of direction after he discovered that the case of Jesus would not be handled by the High Priests, but by Pilate (Matthew 27:1-10). *(For Matt. 21:33-43, see the Twentieth Sunday after Pentecost.)*

HOMILETICAL REFLECTIONS

As I write these words, Robert S. McNamara's book describing his serious regrets about what he did during the Vietnam War, is garnering considerable attention (*In Retrospect: The Tragedy and Lessons of Vietnam* [New York: Random House, 1995]). It is moving to see a man of his stature and accomplishments weeping in public over actions committed thirty years ago. Many of us tried then to get him to change his mind. Many worked very hard to change the course of American policy with respect to Southeast Asia and, although eventually those efforts were successful, too many people died before there was evidence that any change would come.

Often the call to change course goes unheeded. There is no room for self-righteousness, even when things do eventually turn out the way we had hoped. Injustice is too rampant within us, around us, both in the church and in our nation, for any of us to become complacent.

It is a great temptation to assume that we are, of course, the child working faithfully in the vineyard. Everyone else is skiing in winter or playing golf in summer. The issues are never quite that simple. For whatever our verbal commitments may be and whatever ways we may use to justify our own existence, the judgment of the Lord is always more thorough than is our own, but at the same time much more generous than we are to ourselves.

These texts do remind us of a fundamental truth of human existence. Some years ago, a case of a young, autistic girl was described in which the turning point in the healing process for her came when each member of the therapeutic team individually said to the little girl, "I am sorry, very sorry." As the case unfolded, it became evident that these were words her parents refused to say to her. As the little girl realized her parents' failings, she clammed up more and more, and no one could open up the secret to her life until the magic words "I'm sorry" were spoken to her by people that had begun to matter to her. The way of righteousness and the path of justice can only open up to us if we turn away, repent, and decide to walk on the path that leads to life.

Twentieth Sunday after Pentecost
Twenty-Seventh Sunday in Ordinary Time
Proper 23

Lectionary	First Lesson	Psalm	Second Lesson	Gospel
Revised Common	Isa. 25:1-9	Psalm 23	Phil. 4:1-9	Matt. 22:1-14
Episcopal (BCP)	Isa. 25:1-9	Psalm 23	Phil. 4:4-13	Matt. 22:1-14
Roman Catholic	Isa. 5:1-7	Ps. 80:9, 12-16, 19-20	Phil. 4:6-9	Matt. 21:33-43
Lutheran (LBW)	Isa. 5:1-7	Ps. 80:7-14	Phil. 3:12-21	Matt. 21:33-43

FIRST LESSON: ISAIAH 5:1-7; 25:1-9

Some consider the beautiful song of **Isaiah 5:1-7** a parable; perhaps one of the earliest parables that has come down to us in holy literature. Others would treat it as an allegory. In any case, it is a great literary masterpiece, describing the impatience of Yahweh with the people and Yahweh's intention to let the vineyard go to waste.

Few things are as sad to behold as a field untended or a vineyard neglected. The fruit that the master of the vineyard expects is justice. That is clear from the last verse (7), where the full indictment against the vineyard is articulated. Both parts of the sentence compliment each other. They are parallel and mean virtually the same thing.

The strength of a parable (or as the Hebrews would call it, a *mashal*) is that while it impales its object and severely condemns the one who is in mind, it also allows you the option of simply saying, "The story does not apply to me." Those in Israel or Judah who did, in fact, produce righteousness and justice, could blithely say, "This does not apply to me." The parable describes in practical, everyday terms a spiritual truth. In this case, it is God's indictment of Judah, which has been short on justice. The punishment of God will come, for the vineyard belongs to the Lord of Hosts, and both the people of Israel and the people of Judah are the plant that Yahweh cherished. The love of God cannot go on incessantly without reaping some response.

Isaiah 25 also deals with the future, but sounds a positive note and stresses the banquet theme. Other nations will join in the celebration of the covenant that Yahweh has with the people, and they will take note of the way in which God provides for the people and rewards them for their faithfulness (see the Twenty-First Sunday after Pentecost).

EPISTLE: PHILIPPIANS 3:12-21; 4:1-13

Philippians 3:12-21. Paul's perspective on life in Christ is here articulated in detail. It is driven by one consuming passion: "That I may gain Christ" (Phil. 3:8), be found in his righteousness (3:9), and to know Christ and the power of his resurrection and thus share both in Christ's death and his resurrection. This hope must not be extinguished by the false assumption that it has been already realized. Paul avoids the trap of thinking he "has made it" or has already attained his goals. He presses on toward that end—and he does so because Jesus has already "made him his own" (v. 2).

Three times Paul calls his readers his "brothers and sisters" (3:13, 17; 4:1). He first assures them that he has not yet achieved the status of perfection and he then urges them to imitate him.

In the summary paragraph (vv. 17-21), Paul describes the fate of those whose God is their belly, those who live as enemies of Christ. But he does so without any gloating—it is done with tears (v. 18). This earmark of Paul's ministry (2 Cor. 2:4; Acts 20:31, 37) is somewhat embarrassing to us and we certainly do not imitate him in that regard. Most of us have been trained to keep our cool, to tightly control our emotions, especially in public. Did not a public display of tears lose Edmund Muskie critical support in his bid for the presidency of the United States?

Paul, however, is in touch with the gospel. Just as Jesus could weep over the city of Jerusalem (Luke 19:41), which did not know how to work for peace, and at the grave of Lazarus, his friend who had died (John 11:35), so Paul's tears spring from his compassion for those who are "enemies of Christ." They have their minds set on earthly things—and Paul knows how empty, how very futile, such an investment turns out to be. Earthly things are not in themselves bad, they simply promise more than they deliver—always. They fail to satisfy, even on this earth, to say nothing of the beyond where none of those earthly things can enter.

Two contrasts dominate this paragraph: two commonwealths, the one consisting of the enemies of Christ and the other the commonwealth in heaven headed by "our Savior, the Lord Jesus Christ." It is on him that our hope is focused and he will change our lowly body to be like his glorious body. The reign of Christ and the commonwealth (*politeuma*) to which we belong has an orientation not centered on the physical needs of the belly or the things that perish.

The Greek world had hundreds of blueprints of how people were to live together. Plato's *Republic* is perhaps the most enduring and the most worthy of reflection. Paul, surely aware of many efforts in the Greco-Roman world to build human societies, pits the rule of Christ over against any other efforts to exercise sovereignty over people's lives. While this particular sentence can lead us to irrelevant other-worldliness, Paul's agenda just before that and immediately after it presents a very well-rounded approach.

Philippians 4:1-13. Given the headaches that many Christians in churches which Paul had founded caused him, one can understand that he prayed for them—God knows they needed his prayers! But Paul also describes his audience as "beloved brothers and sisters"(3:13, 17; 4:1). The church is above all a family, a close-knit, functioning family in which people care for each other. Paul does not hesitate to say how he misses his brothers and sisters in Christ. They are, he continues, "my joy and crown." When the mission of the church is defined as a collaboration in joy (2 Cor. 1:24) then all members become important. All are a source of joy and of pride.

But here in Philippi there are also concrete problems. People don't seem to get along. To those people, whom he names, he suggests that they learn to "think along the same lines in the Lord" (4:2). Paul addresses a "yokefellow," a term used in classical Greek for marriage partner. Could it be that Paul's wife is in Philippi? Some early church leaders have suggested this, but most commentators find such a notion a bit too radical.

The preposition *sum* appears here four times in v. 3 alone. Paul visualizes the church as a *sym*phony and it is hard to conceive of a symphony performing effectively or beautifully when each person plays his or her own score, fights with the others, goes his or her own way, does not look at the conductor, or refuses to listen to the others. Paul is proud of his co-workers (fourteen of whom he mentions by name, four fellow prisoners, two fellow soldiers, two fellow slaves), whose names are written in the book of life. As George Caird once wrote: "Paul never had any assistants or underlings—only partners and colleagues."

Three themes dominate the remaining verses of this chapter: joy, peace, and being carefree. "Don't worry," Paul says crisply. How often we say that to others or have it said to us! Saying those words is easy, but it is more difficult to know how one can turn such advice into action. When you need something, ask God for it. The same advice seems to be found in Jesus' words, "Take no thought for the morrow"; the Johannine literature admonishes that community also to pray specifically for what one needs and it will be given (John 14:13; 1 John 5:14). A different world than the one we live in today! At the same time, we are told anxiety is good to a certain point and the best performers are those who have stage fright. Fretting and worry are, however, fundamentally denials that God exists or that God cares. For Paul, excessive worrying is an expression of unbelief.

The ultimate protection against worry is the peace of God. Note Paul's terminology, which centers on the peace of God, which is like the Godself, much bigger than our comprehension. It can be in charge of thoughts and rational planning, as well as feelings, the emotional part of each of us. The peace of God stands as guardian at the door and determines what shall enter.

An insertion beginning with "finally" in v. 8 is packed with the things with which the Philippians are encouraged to "fill" their minds:

- everything that is true
- everything that is noble
- everything that is good and pure
- everything we love and honor
- everything that can be thought virtuous or worthy of praise.

Paul urges them to persevere in what they have learned, received, heard from, and seen in him. The English translations begin the sentence with "then," which would seem to imply that if these conditions are met, the God of peace will be with them. But that is not what Paul says.

For Paul the description of God as the God of Peace is foundational. Although Christians do not worship a different God than do the Jews, early Christians made certain affirmations about God or put emphasis on certain attributes of God not before seen. Such is the case with the description of God as a God of peace. The term *peace* is connected with God at many places in the Hebrew Bible, and God is named "peace" at one place (Judges 6:24). God makes peace, so Isaiah says, using the word normally used for God's creating power (45:7; 60:17; 66:12).

But it is left for the early church to settle on the designation: the God of peace. This means that God is not a God of war (cf. Exod. 15:3). Peace characterizes God's activity—not war. God brings peace because it is in the very nature of God to do so. It is no surprise that Paul unites in this one paragraph the peace of God and the God of peace. The two obviously are closely tied to each other and it is impossible to imagine the peace of God if God is not a God of peace. From Paul's earliest epistle (1 Thess. 5:23), to this, one of his last, Paul serves a God of peace and it is therefore critically important that the community at Philippi recognize the presence of the God of peace among them. Therein lies also the solution to inner personal peace. There is no place for fretting and worrying when one serves the God of peace.

GOSPEL: MATTHEW 21:33-43

This parable is one of three found in three of the Gospels: Mark, Luke, and Matthew; evidently it spoke to issues alive in all three communities. In Matthew's redemptive history scheme this parable highlights a major conviction of his community: God has taken the vineyard, the kingdom of God, from Israel and transferred it to a mysterious nation (v. 43). The outlines of the story are clearly portrayed. One can also see why Jewish Christians in Galilee, living side by side with Jews who did not accept Jesus as Messiah, could relish a story like this. All the messengers sent by the owner of the vineyard are mocked or killed. The farmers of the vineyard think they owe no one anything. Finally, when the landowner sends his son, he is thrown outside the vineyard and killed. The farmers in the audience must have chuckled to themselves.

The city dwellers, however, also get a piece of the action. The illustration of the stone rejected by the builders was a commonplace. Palestine is a land of many stones. When you go to see the excavations near the Western Wall in Jerusalem, you encounter an enormous stone, measuring forty-two feet long, eleven feet high, and ten feet wide. There are three other oversized stones on the site where the temple rested. When Herod laid the foundations for the temple between 10 and 20 B.C.E., these stones were possibly at first rejected because of their enormous size. Perhaps Herod insisted that the foundation for the temple must be strong and invincible and insisted that nothing would do but these stones. In any case, this story, along with others, would have circulated among the building trades, where Jesus first heard about them, and many would have come to admire this magnificent cornerstone.

But eighty years later, such building feats would be known only through hearsay. What they knew firsthand was the destruction of the temple and the total defeat of the Jews by the Romans in 66–73 C.E. This parable views that defeat as the judgment and punishment of a long-suffering God who would give up and even offer up God's Son.

Strictly speaking, it is difficult to see anything in this parable but a supersession theology, which assumes that God's role for the Jews is over. The vineyard now belongs to the Christians, it seems to say. And while that idea may not have been far from Matthew's mind, we have no choice but to reject it. God never utterly rejects the people created by Divine decree; God never deserts the chosen peoples. That plural is vitally important.

Walbert Bühlmann, for many years a missionary, a leader in interfaith dialogue in the Vatican, and a theologian of peace, once published a book titled *The Chosen Peoples* (London: St. Paul Publications, 1988), which carries an important message. God chooses peoples to carry out special missions and tasks and may punish them when they are unfaithful and turn the commission over to others. But repeatedly God returns to the people created and called and loved always. Paul saw that when he penned Romans 9–11; the overall message of Matthew's Gospel is the same.

We live today as if the landowner will never return. Our earth is ravaged by human greed. We live as if it belongs to us and we can do with it as we like. In the meantime, irreparable damage is being done to our ecosystem which, if not reversed, will have ominous consequences. There are not unlimited amounts of fish in our oceans. We are no better than the farmers in this parable, and thus have no reason to imagine that judgment will not come and the vineyard be taken away from us.

(For Matt. 22:1-14, see the Twenty-First Sunday after Pentecost.)

Twenty-First Sunday after Pentecost
Twenty-Eighth Sunday in Ordinary Time
Proper 24

Lectionary	First Lesson	Psalm	Second Lesson	Gospel
Revised Common	Isa. 45:1-7	Ps. 96:1-9, (10-13)	I Thess. 1:1-10	Matt. 22:15-22
Episcopal (BCP)	Isa. 45:1-7	Psalm 96 *or* 96:1-9	I Thess. 1:1-10	Matt. 22:15-22
Roman Catholic	Isa. 25:6-10a	Ps. 23:1-6	Phil. 4:12-14, 19-20	Matt. 22:1-14 *or* 22:1-10
Lutheran (LBW)	Isa. 25:6-9	Psalm 23	Phil. 4:4-13	Matt. 22:1-10 (11-14)

FIRST LESSON: ISAIAH 25:6-10A; 45:1-7

In this oracle from **Isaiah 25:6-10a**, the prophet makes three affirmations about God and uses three images to describe the salvation that God brings to the people. The first is the image of a feast, depicted in mouth-watering terms, in which the Lord of Hosts (generally the military term or the term of deliverance used for God) is the host (v. 6). The second image is the image of destruction focused on death. God will swallow up death forever and the shroud of death, which lies over all people, will be removed (v. 7). Finally, Isaiah speaks specifically about the Lord God wiping away the tears from all faces (v. 8).

This poignant and moving image of the Lord God wiping away tears caught the imagination of several biblical writers and has, of course, been a source of great comfort to many humans throughout the centuries. When life is engulfed in grief and sorrow, this reality speaks to the heart.

No distant God this, no unmoved deity showing greatness by refusing to be moved by human pain. This is a God who takes a handkerchief and wipes the tears from those who are grieving. No wonder that in the Gospels, when Jesus walks among his people, he is noted for his compassion in removing, rather than inflicting, pain and grief. People who are called "the Great" in history have often been noted for their military prowess, the number of people they have killed; not so with Jesus.

Little wonder as well that the book of Revelation also picks up this motif and depicts God as the one who removes the tears from all faces (5:5; 7:17; 21:4). The writer summarizes all of these things by describing God, who is worth waiting for, a God who saves the people, and as the one who brings gladness and joy in Divine salvation. The final line is a promise that the hand of the Lord will rest on this mountain, a beautiful way of saying that God's presence will never be removed from the people of God.

Isaiah 45:1-7. Isaiah 45 speaks of the Lord's choice of Cyrus, a pagan king, to be the messiah, the anointed one. It is through Cyrus—specifically through his strong right arm—that God will subdue nations and strip kings of their robes. Doors of bronze will be broken in pieces, bars of iron will be cut, all of this so that "You may know that it is I, the LORD, the God of Israel, who call you by your name" (45:3). It is precisely for the sake of Jacob and of Israel that God calls Cyrus to do God's work. This does not in any way diminish the importance of the fact that there is no God besides Yahweh. It is Yahweh who arms Cyrus, even though Cyrus may not be aware of it.

Fundamental to both Judaism and Christianity, as well as to Islam, is the oneness of God. There is none beside God. God is the One who created light and created darkness, who also makes *shalom*. The word in 45:7 that is translated "weal" is the Hebrew word *shalom*, which means prosperity or wholeness. It is one of the most important texts of the Hebrew Bible, because it describes God as not only the author of *shalom*, but also the creator of woe or chaos (but compare Isa. 45:18-19).

The remarkable way in which nationalistic hopes of the early Israelites were curbed is shown through this statement that God will choose Cyrus, king of their traditional enemy, to achieve the Divine will and purposes. Such a prediction must not have helped Isaiah's popularity rating but it does illustrate something of the inclusiveness of the prophet. The modern Israeli writer, A. B. Yehoshua, once described the "problem of the Jews [is] that they have no borders and it has been thus from the beginning of history" (*Jerusalem Post Magazine*, 28 April 1995). When one considers the extraordinary capacity of Jews to survive in history, perhaps Isaiah's point is that the Jews as God's chosen people have no borders, because God does not get caught up in borders either. Come to think of it, Jesus too strode across the borders between Judea and Samaria, and the church has survived as well in large part because in Christ there is neither Jew nor Greek, and traditional boundaries are removed. To a certain extent, borders are important to build a strong people and a strong personality. At the same time what are we to make of Cyrus, the messiah?

SECOND LESSON: PHILIPPIANS 4:12-14, 19-20; I THESSALONIANS 1:1-10

Philippians 4:12-14, 19-20. The Philippian letter, as already noted, is one of the most profound epistles written by Paul. In it issues of life and death confront the gospel. As Paul draws to the conclusion of this letter, he seeks to express his thanks to the Philippians for what they have done for him, but also to make it plain to them that he has a measure of independence. He remains a free man, unbeholden to anyone. So, his expressions of thanks and his statement that he is self-sufficient stand side by side.

Two dimensions that are highlighted in this segment are, first, Paul's interest in the peace of God (v. 7), which he describes as that which is beyond comprehension, and, second, his prayer that the peace of God may hold their hearts and thoughts in custody, or bondage, in Christ Jesus. The imagery here is very vivid and comes out of the practice of guarding and protecting prisoners. It is quite likely that Paul saw himself as "imprisoned" by the peace of God, and he wishes this to be their fate as well. In the next sentence, he switches the imagery and he prays that the God of peace may be with them.

The theology of peace, which is so strongly represented now among Christian theologians, pervades, of course, both the writings of the early Hebrews and that of the early Christian community. Ulrich Mauser has, in his *Gospel of Peace* (Louisville: Westminster/John Knox, 1992), shown brilliantly how central this concept of peace is to the gospel. Paul, in his statements in this section, whether it be v. 11, "I have learned to be self sufficient," or whether it is that he is enabled to do all things, "empowered to do all things through the one who gives him power" (v. 13), demonstrates that he has found the secret of a fulfilled and purposeful life.

His Stoic contemporaries, and certainly his Cynic friends, would have scoffed at this kind of self-sufficiency, which comes from his union with Christ. How can one be independent if one's life is totally absorbed and totally stitched together with that of a master, even if he is called Jesus? But this precisely is the richness of the gospel, as Paul described it here, writing from his prison cell to the Philippians. Some may, of course, cast it aside as ranting and raving and as something that is profoundly removed from the realm of reality. Let the record speak for itself, and let Paul's own contribution to Western civilization and to the spiritual development of many people be its own advocate.

1 Thessalonians 1:1-10 strikes a similar note. Coming as it does at the very beginning of Paul's own writings, it contains the usual praise that often comes at the beginning of an epistle. Paul praises his readers, confident that they are people in whom the gospel is bearing fruit.

In this section, it is most unusual that in v. 3, Paul, after having told them that he thanks God for each one of them continually, specifies the three dimensions of their life for which he is grateful. He specifically mentions these to God the Father in his prayers: faith, which shows itself in action; love, which is demonstrated through its labor; and hope, which is characterized by its steadfastness.

In each instance, Paul draws together things that often are separated from each other: faith and works, love and labor, and hope and certainty or steadfastness. But this is precisely the strength of Paul's view of the Christian life. This is what he observes in the Thessalonian Christians and it is a product of their having accepted the word of God in power when it was proclaimed to them. The Holy Spirit did her gracious work among them.

The evidence is apparent from many perspectives. In the last part of this introduction to the Thessalonian letter, he commends them for having followed Paul's example (note this aspect also appears in Phil. 4:9), and they received the word of God with great suffering (1 Thess. 1:6). At the same time, this grave suffering was united with the joy that they had in the Holy Spirit, and by bringing these two together, they became models for all the believers in that area. So, the word of the Lord rang out throughout that region, and their faith became the talk of the area.

Finally, he describes their reversal from idol worship to become servants of the living and the true God. Part of their faith and part of this reversal means to wait expectantly for the appearance from heaven of Jesus, who will deliver them from the terrors of judgment to come. It is the resurrection from the dead of this Jesus that provides the power to transform human lives.

GOSPEL: MATTHEW 22:1-14

This Parable of the Marriage Feast is found in a slightly different form in Luke 14:15-24. It develops in three stages. The first is the invitation to the wedding banquet. Slaves are sent out who make two special trips to tell the people who are invited that everything is ready, the dinner has been prepared, the meat has been slaughtered, and to urge them to come to the wedding banquet. The first time the invitees simply will not come, but the second time they make light of the invitation, their own occupations take precedence; some seize, mistreat, and even kill the slaves.

It is, obviously, difficult to understand that people would be killed simply for inviting others to a feast. No doubt, the author of the Gospel is reading into this some of the events of his own lifetime. The urgency of the invitation is stressed by the repetition of everything being prepared or everything being ready (v. 4), and the repetition again in v. 8 that the wedding is ready, but those who were invited were not worthy.

The question of who is worthy to be invited to the wedding is an intriguing one because, when the first and second round of invitations do not yield results, the troops are sent out to destroy the murderers and burn their city. After that happened, the slaves again are sent on their mission and they go into the main streets and invite everyone to come. Now they gathered "both good and bad" so the wedding hall was filled with guests. Part of the point of the parable surely is that the wedding invitation, although going out to everyone, still dictates that the person coming to the wedding will be properly attired. It was customary then that the wedding robe was supplied to the guest if she or he does not come with one. In this case, the person must have rejected the offer of a wedding robe, thus insulting the host. This is a serious breach of etiquette and the king, somewhat facetiously, calls him a friend and asks him "How did you get in here without a wedding garment?" Obviously, the impolite, if not rude, guest cannot answer the question and, therefore, he is punished accordingly.

As it stands, the parable could hardly go back to Jesus. It does not reflect his spirit and, above all, it is in sharp contrast to the generosity of the banquet described in Isaiah 45. No doubt, however, it reflects the Matthean community's attempt to deal with the events that took place during the years 66 to 70 C.E., when the city of Jerusalem was, in fact, destroyed. Garments have a strong, symbolic character in the New Testament. In this case, the parable is clearly meant to draw more tightly the limits of the Christian community and to define more precisely who is in and who is out. This may be important in certain stages of history, but it is always dangerous in a community that is defined basically by inclusiveness, as is the community of Jesus.

Invitations to feasts, banquets, and weddings are carefully controlled. It can be no other way. In Matthew's community, this parable makes the strong point that certain conditions must be met to be able to attend the feast. Matthew needed to draw limits and define boundaries between Jew and Christian, Cynic and Christian.

The feast that he describes is meant to be an inclusive one, since "both good and bad" sit at table together. But the point of this parable, according to Matthew, is that "many are invited but few are chosen." Note the choosing is done not by the host but by those who decline the invitation. Thus did Matthew try to encourage his people in the face of the small numbers of people joining the Christian movement.

(For Matt. 22:15-22, see the Twenty-Second Sunday after Pentecost.)

HOMILETICAL REFLECTIONS

Douglas John Hall has recently been reminding us that the age of Christendom is over in the West and that it is time that our church structures recognize that. We no longer hold the key to political dominance over our neighbors.

Rather than causing us gloom or discouragement, I suggest that we consider the image of the feast or the banquet—especially, if you will, with Matthew, the wedding banquet. The one word that comes to mind in connection with such an event is *joy*. In our texts, Paul speaks of the Thessalonians receiving the word in tribulation and joy inspired by the Holy Spirit (1 Thess. 1:6).

Joy is not elation, it is not pleasure, it is not even happiness. Joy is, rather, the profound sense of well-being which comes from knowing that we are under the protection and mandate of the God of Love. "Blessed are those who are invited to the wedding supper of the Lamb," writes John in Revelation 19:9. And even more blessed and more joyous are those who accept the invitation. At the wedding of the lamb the bride's adornment is fine linen, clean and shining, signifying the "deeds of justice of God's people" (Rev. 19:8; 15:3-4).

Twenty-Second Sunday after Pentecost
Twenty-Ninth Sunday in Ordinary Time
Proper 25

Lectionary	First Lesson	Psalm	Second Lesson	Gospel
Revised Common	Lev. 19:1-2, 15-18	Psalm 1	1 Thess. 2:1-8	Matt. 22:34-46
Episcopal (BCP)	Exod. 22:21-27	Psalm 1	1 Thess. 2:1-8	Matt. 22:34-46
Roman Catholic	Isa. 45:1, 4-6	Ps. 96:1, 3-5, 7-10	1 Thess. 1:1-5a	Matt. 22:15-21
Lutheran (LBW)	Isa. 45:1-7	Psalm 96	1 Thess. 1:1-5a	Matt. 22:15-21

FIRST LESSON: EXODUS 22:21-27; LEVITICUS 19:1-2, 15-18

Exodus 22:21-27. One problem of every society is how to relate to the marginal people. The code from Exodus describes in detail how to protect the alien from any abuse or wrongdoing. In a similar way, the widow and the orphan, vulnerable as they are in a patriarchal society once their support has been removed, need to be protected. The warning stands that when the oppressed cry out to God, God's wrath will be invoked. This is especially true in the case of lending money.

The person's cloak, taken as collateral, must be restored before the sun goes down so that they have something with which to cover themselves in the night. The forceful mandate overall is that justice shall be observed in dealing with those people who have no protection of their own. (For more on these verses, see the Twenty-Third Sunday after Pentecost.)

Leviticus 19:1-2, 15-18. The Leviticus material strengthens this even more in that the Israelites are reminded that God is holy and that their own behavior also must be patterned in this respect on God's. They are to show respect for their parents and to keep the Sabbath. Furthermore, the law against idol worship and making graven images is enforced by the solemn theological sanction: "I am the LORD your God."

Again, more concretely, the specific way in which justice is administered is strengthened by an appeal for impartiality. No special favor is allowed for the powerful, the great, or the rich; justice is to be the only criterion on which judgment is based.

Further protection comes in that the slanderer is sharply admonished. Slander is to speak not only things that are false; it is to speak things that, even though they may be true, should not be told. The ones who spill the blood of their neighbors are also admonished.

In all of this, the fundamental rule is that no hate is to be allowed in your heart toward any of your neighbors or your kin, and the words, "or you will incur guilt yourself," confirms that the mandate to reprove the neighbor is central to Israel's existence. It was indeed practiced widely and affirmed throughout the centuries. The best protection for the community is to be forthright with your neighbor and to reprove them. When that reproof is lacking, the person who is aware of the sin being committed incurs guilt.

Jesus, moreover, confirms this mandate in Matthew 18:15. It rests on the firm conviction that the community exists only when people take responsibility for each other's actions. The danger of incurring guilt upon oneself comes, according to Jewish teaching, when you do not intervene or try to assist your colleagues in overcoming temptation or sin. The commandment, then, to love your neighbor "as yourself" not only does away with all need for vengeance, all tendency to bear a grudge, but recognizes that your life is inextricably bound up with that of your neighbor.

There is no command for self-love here, or indeed anywhere in the Bible. Rather, the Hebrews believed that you should love your neighbor because your neighbor is the same as, or at least a part of yourself.

The word *self*, which we moderns have imperiously made into a noun, existed only as a pronoun in ancient society and into the modern age. The odyssey of the self-centered self, to cite the title of Robert Fitch's important book, ultimately leads to the enthronement of the self as God. After that the well runs dry. There is a profound richness, therefore, in this commandment to love the neighbor, because it demonstrates the way in which our lives are inextricably bound up with each other.

As soon as an atomic reactor malfunctions in Chernobyl, virtually the whole world is affected by it. The eruption of a volcano in the state of Washington or in the Philippines affects the climate over the whole world. In this way, no one really is bound only unto himself or herself.

(For Isa. 45:1-7, see the Twenty-First Sunday after Pentecost.)

SECOND LESSON: I THESSALONIANS 2:1-8

1 Thessalonians is uniformly treated as a genuine Pauline letter, and scholars generally recognize it as among his earliest writings. Paul's dominant theme in this section, which has been sudied considerably, is to advise his readers not to become alarmed or to "lose their heads." They are not to be swept away by some letter or some pronouncement that claims to have come from Paul and alleges that the Day of the Lord is already here. He is trying to prevent them from being deceived.

The word *enemy* (or, the man doomed to perdition) is the main category, and over against that stands the restrainer (v. 7). Paul views human history as a contest between good and evil, and the evil one is being restrained from wreaking total destruction upon the human scene. According to Paul, there is a timetable, certain things have to happen before the Lord returns, but when the evil one is totally unveiled, the Lord Jesus will destroy by the breath of his mouth and annihilate by the radiance of his coming.

The presence of that wicked man is, he firmly believes, the work of Satan. Satan has been much discussed in recent literature. Elaine Pagels, in *The Origin of Satan* (New York: Random House, 1995), has written movingly about the prominence of the evil one, Satan, in early Christian sources and especially the way in which that has been used in later Christianity. She is correct that much harm can be done by invoking the satanic. At the same time, one must raise the question whether the early Christian writers may not have been more realistic than those who argue that human history is characterized primarily by good and that the demonic has no place.

Fundamental to Paul's view is the work of the restrainer. He receives that from the stories of Jesus, who never failed to confront the demonic and who always came out triumphant over demonic powers. Consequently, one could suggest that in Christian tradition the biggest problem has not been the introduction of the category of the demonic; rather, it is our failure to comprehend and appropriate the power of Jesus to drive out demons. Above all, we fail as a community committed to Christ to repeat that effective exorcism. At any rate, Paul's message is clear and as important to us as then: Beware of those who seek to deceive you.

(For 1 Thess. 1:1-5, see the Twenty-First Sunday after Pentecost.)

GOSPEL: MATTHEW 22:15-21, 34-46

In Matthew 22, four questions are put to Jesus; today's lessons deal with two of these. In the first question, the Herodians and Pharisees ask Jesus about paying tribute to Caesar; in the third question, the Pharisees ask, "What is the greatest commandment of the law?"

In the first instance, Matthew tells us that the Pharisees were seeking to "trip him up." Indeed, in his reply, Jesus asks, "Why do you seek to tempt me or test me?" (v. 18). The third question is already introduced by Matthew as a testing or temptation (v. 35) and it has none of the unctuous flattery found in the first one. These questions address two critical issues of human existence: What do we owe to governmental authorities? What are the limits of the demands the body politic can make on us and under what circumstances do we dissent from obeying Caesar? The second question deals with the nature of our obligation to God. If we owe the state some respect and obedience, our obligation to God must also be discussed. It is discharged by love.

The context of these discussions must be seen as the years between 70–90 C.E., when the Matthean community was attempting to regroup after the destruction of the temple (70 C.E.) and the total routing of all Jewish resistance by the Romans with the fall of Masada (73 C.E.). The Jews who had been routed from Jerusalem had settled in Galilee and were busy reestablishing their priorities in the communities where they were inevitably thrown into dialogue with Christians. The Pharisees were central figures of leadership among the Jews and they had much to do to try to define the relationships with Christians during these days. The Christians likewise needed to consider urgently their relationship to Jews. The baiting and sparring that went on between the two groups may be accurately reflected in Matthew's narrative.

The same issues with respect to Caesar may have been operative and debated during the time of Jesus. Jesus had to decide whether to adopt the Pharisaic position and separate religion as much as possible from the state or to try to build once more a theocracy in which God alone rules and all kingly powers are then relativized in ways that make all kings uncomfortable on their thrones. For states believe that their citizens owe them not only taxes but also (in modern times) one's life in military service when needed.

For Jesus the issue is clear: Undeterred by their fawning flattery he asks them, "Why do you tempt me, hypocrites? Show me the tribute coin." It is typical of Jesus to employ the Socratic method; it was also a good rabbinic teaching technique to throw a question back to his interrogators, "Whose image and superscription does it bear?" It is possible that they had to scamper away to get a coin, for they would not carry it and defile themselves with a graven image. But for Jesus the evidence is unambiguous. If you carry Caesar's coins, you must pay back to Caesar what he has given to you.

At the same time, this is no blanket endorsement of the rights of government. The statement, "pay back to God what is God's" puts all human obligations into perspective. Norman Gottwald notes that Gandhi already saw this better than most Christians. As Gandhi put it, "Jesus did render unto Caesar that which was Caesar's. He gave the devil his dues! By his answer of 'noncooperation' Jesus showed himself a 'prince of politicians.'"

The third question in the series is a commonplace topic among teacher and students: What is the greatest thing in the world? What is the most important or the greatest commandment? In Scripture, we find this question addressed in 1 Corinthians 13 and noted implicitly in many other places. The phrasing of the question is based on the respect they had for the way he handled the previous question and Jesus does not disappoint them. He not only answers their question but goes on: The greatest commandment is to love the Lord God. . . . This is the greatest and the first commandment. But the second one has equal weight: Love your neighbor for your neighbor is just like you are. All the law and the prophets hang or depend upon these two.

Jesus shows up here as a brilliant Jewish teacher. He builds solidly on his own faith and repeats sacred texts to support his position. He also shows himself sensitive to the needs of the common people—not just to the scholastic interests of lawyers and theologians. In the two answers given to two critical human questions, Jesus gave out sound pastoral advice. I sometimes wonder what human history might have been like if we had spent as much money, time, and energy on cultivating love for God and neighbor as we do on romantic love. Neither Jesus or Paul ever spent much time on romantic love or sexual love. Yet what they said is basic to true love for it is basic to all relationships.

For Jesus, the main issue of life is whether one can give oneself wholly to God and then love the neighbor as deeply as one loves oneself. It is surely the greatest tribute one can pay him as a teacher to note that as profound as he was as a teacher, he was equally adept at helping people kindle such love for God among each other and to practice neighborly love. Here we are at the very foundation of the church and to understand these things means that we have come a long way in understanding what it means to be the people of God.

HOMILETICAL REFLECTIONS

In many ways, the most important category in the religious life for both Jews and Christians is justice. Here, in these sections of holy writings, we are reminded again of the God of justice and that we cannot evade the coming of justice. Better than that, we are reminded that a community can begin the process of executing justice, or of administering justice, not only to its own adherents, but to those who live on the fringes of the community, the alien or the neighbor. Simultaneously, there is an invitation here to participate in the generosity and compassion of God. Ironically, the most difficult story to incorporate into our thinking here is the parable from Matthew 22 (see the Twenty-First Sunday after Pentecost).

In a recent study of the concept of vengeance in the Bible, a Dutch scholar concludes that the view of vengeance is exactly the same in the

Old Testament as it is in the New. That is a little hard to accept when we recall that one psalm looks forward to the time when the righteous one will rejoice when he sees the vengeance and will bathe his feet in the blood of the wicked (Ps. 58:10). In sharp contrast is the picture of Jesus, according to the Fourth Gospel, washing the feet of Judas and the other disciples, none of whom would prove to be particularly helpful, even if we do not classify them as the enemies of Jesus.

Fundamentally, both Jews and Christians defer the subject of vengeance to God, fully expecting God to administer justice. Human vengeance, therefore, has no place among the people of God. Our job is to wait, to wait for God. In that context, it is easy to be deceived by false prophets, by evil, well-meaning, or even ignorant, people. That problem goes back at least to the very early years of Paul's own ministry, if not to Jesus himself. Alertness, then, is the primary Christian virtue—to stay awake, to keep one's mind active, and, above all, to think through matters of value and matters of importance in the context of the community.

Here it may be well to remind ourselves that, while we focus on many sins and irregularities, one of the fundamental problems of human existence is slander. It is a sin that wreaks devastation upon community life and destroys individuals, not just their reputations. Jewish law, therefore, severely condemns it. Jesus, as well as other New Testament writers, also speaks about the harm that can be committed by the tongue. We do well to remind ourselves that slander involves not only telling false tales, but also telling stories that may be true but deserve not to be told. In our society, where information, disinformation, misinformation, and all kinds of propaganda are repeatedly reported as truth, it would not harm the Christian church to be vigilant and to try to rid itself of the sin of slander and seek instead to introduce the practice of loving, warm rebuke spoken in love. A Hebrew sage already noted that boldly reproving someone is to "make peace" (Prov. 10:10). When Jesus spoke his blessing upon the peacemakers and promised them the highest possible status, to be called a child of God, he affirmed an approach central to Jewish community and practiced with considerable energy by the Jewish community of the new covenant at Qumran.

Twenty-Third Sunday after Pentecost
Thirtieth Sunday in Ordinary Time
Proper 26

Lectionary	First Lesson	Psalm	Second Lesson	Gospel
Revised Common	Micah 3:5-12	Psalm 43	I Thess. 2:9-13	Matt. 23:1-12
Episcopal (BCP)	Micah 3:5-12	Psalm 43	I Thess. 2:9-13, 17-20	Matt. 23:1-12
Roman Catholic	Exod. 22:20-26	Ps. 18:2-4, 47-51	I Thess. 1:5b-10	Matt. 22:34-40
Lutheran (LBW)	Lev. 19:1-2, 15-18	Psalm 1	I Thess. 1:5b-10	Matt. 22:34-40 (41-46)

EXEGETICAL OBSERVATIONS

The common theme of our readings is the implementation of the law that calls for loving the neighbor as yourself. The three readings from the Hebrew Bible differ in that two are legal codes (Exod. 22:20-26; Lev. 19:1-2, 15-18), the other a prophetic critique of how the religious and political leaders are doing (Micah 3:5-12). A view is provided into the life of the earliest community at Thessalonica (1 Thess. 1:5-10; 2:9-13, 17-20). Two selections from Matthew, one dealing with the critique the Matthean community has of the Pharisees of their day (23:1-12), and one a discussion Jesus had with the Pharisees about the love command (22:34-40), show how the quest for integrity continues among God's people.

While the selections from the Hebrew Bible take us back into the eighth century before the time of Christ, also referred to as the common era, and deal with the plight of the vulnerable, the material from the epistle deals more directly with the way the church deals with potential adherents. Paul, as a leader in the early church, lays out some fundamental guidelines on how to deal with people. There is then a superb opportunity to relate the content of the word in the first instance to the role of the church's representatives, minister or lay, the one proclaiming the good news. Both Micah and Paul invite us to allow the light of the gospel to shine upon our motivations, our methods, and the way we exercise power as Christians from the pulpit or the pew.

FIRST LESSON: EXODUS 22:20-26; MICAH 3:5-12

Exodus 22:20-26. This unit from the covenant code begins with a sharp interdiction against sacrificing to other gods. The ban, or *herem*, is more fully described in Joshua 6:17-19. It has been applied to Jericho for centuries and even today it has been suggested that religious Jews have less difficulty turning the city of Jericho back to the Palestinians because no Jew would want to live there. The ban from Jericho has never been removed.

The main focus of the regulations is the protection of the stranger, the widow, and the orphans. God is here depicted as one who hears the cries of these people most vulnerable to oppression. God's retribution will be swift and devastating. Moreover, the practice of usury is also condemned for members of the people, the poor especially are to be protected from this practice. To take a cloak as collateral is allowed if it is returned before nightfall. The nights in Palestine are cold and a night's sleep under a warm cover is a right of God's children. The cry of those without blankets will be heard.

The sanctions of these ethical mandates are historical and theological. Historically, the people of Israel are reminded that they were once strangers; God heard their cry when they were oppressed in Egypt and will hear the cry of those whom they in turn oppress. Theologically, God is not lenient toward those who worship other gods; the anger of God can flare up and God "will kill you with the sword" (22:24).

But most important is that God listens to those who cry out for help, a point made twice in this brief section (vv. 23, 27). The covenant made by God is no indelible right and is reciprocal. In particular, it is not meant to be interpreted as a special status that allows, with impunity, oppression of others.

Emil Fackenheim, a Canadian philosopher now living in Israel, has recently declared, "Let this country survive, even if it means that we must be oppressors. Is there an alternative? We are under siege. Is oppression of Arabs by the present state of Israel the price that has to be paid for survival?" *(Jerusalem Post Magazine,* 31 March 1995). We can be sure that God hears even the cries of Palestinians. For God's fullness of pity is not restricted to great throngs of people or even chosen peoples but is directed to those who try to sleep and have nothing in which to wrap themselves. In the ancient Far East, only Israel had a God who would stoop to such modest, but basic, concerns.

Micah 3:5-12. The prophet Micah lived in the Southern Kingdom (Judea) about the time of Isaiah and Amos. He mercilessly criticizes the members of his own guild, the prophets of both Northern and Southern Kingdoms (3:5-8) after he has done the same to the rulers (3:1-4).

The prophets are accused of leading the people astray. The most serious charge is that they keep crying "Peace" as long as they are well fed, but as soon as they have less food, they cry "war." It is a situation in which the amount of pay can adjust the message. Such behavior characterizes a false prophet and applies to local pastors or priests, mass evangelists, and church bureaucrats who adjust their messages to what they think people will want to hear, as much as it applies to cardinals and archbishops. The end is predicted: the messages from God will dry up and they will have nothing to say. The saddest thing that can happen to a community of believers or to a person charged with speaking for God is to be speechless, to have come to an end of a vision to articulate.

But Micah is not like that. "Not so with me, I am full of strength of the breath [spirit] of Yahweh, of justice and courage to declare Jacob's crime to his face and Israel's to his" (v. 8). The last paragraph of this oracle proclaims that a Zion that is built with blood and a Jerusalem built on crime cannot survive. To keep repeating, "Is not Yahweh in our midst? No evil is going to overtake us" is a false security. The chanting song of security of Jerusalem, which has been sung for centuries and is sung again today, cannot avoid the fulfilment of the prediction that "Zion will become ploughland, Jerusalem a heap of rubble, and the temple a wooded height." That happened before and will happen again if justice is not incorporated into the building, Micah says. It happened because political leaders were corrupt and religious leaders were co-opted.

How often has it happened in Jerusalem since those words were written 2,800 years ago? In the meantime, oppression goes on here in this city, Jerusalem, just as it does in New York, Toronto, Chicago, Los Angeles, Washington, and Ottawa.

A reminder. A charge of the first order is laid at the doors of the religious leaders who lack the courage to tell the powerful people the truth. Instead, we tend to repeat the slogans, "Peace, peace," when there really is none. If we soothe our people with lies, we stand under God's judgment.

(For Lev. 19:1-2, 15-18, see the Twenty-Second Sunday after Pentecost.)

SECOND LESSON: I THESSALONIANS 1:5-10; 2:9-13, 17-20

1 Thessalonians 1:5-10 describes the response to the gospel in Thessalonica. It stands in sharp contrast to the failure of the prophets in Micah's day, for Paul's word came to them through power and the same spirit that empowered Micah. They broke with idolatry and converted to serve the living God. Now they wait for the salvation that is to come. (For fuller treatment of these verses, see the Twenty-First Sunday after Pentecost.)

1 Thessalonians 2:9-13, 17-20. Two metaphors drawn from the intimacy of family life become the focus for Paul's model of leadership in the church. The one, "gentle as a nurse with her children" (v. 7), is joined to the metaphor of "the father treating his children" (v. 11), encouraging, admonishing, and bearing witness by example.

In the use of these images, Paul avails himself of the current images used by moral philosophers of his day (so Abraham Malherbe has convincingly shown in his essay, "Exhortation in 1 Thessalonians"). The result is the joining of tenderness and firmness, of nurturing and admonition.

Paul also has to remind them that he was not a burden to them and that he never let his weight be felt. First, he earned his own living and he toiled and labored while among them. Both Jews and Greeks took pride in such an arrangement. Among the Greeks, the argument whether a wise man should charge fees for his instruction goes back at least to Socrates. Those who received pay were considered frauds.

Among the rabbis, such "tent ministry" (or "worker priests," as we call them today), was an established custom. The teacher of the law made his living with a trade on the side. Paul is proud that he would work night and day, rather than be a burden to them (v. 9). Moreover, they (remember Paul was always engaged in team ministry) had been holy, fair, and blameless. There has been nothing underhanded, no trickery, no seduction. Ministry like that is possible although not too frequent. It stands as a strong contrast to what is depicted in Micah and in Matthew. What is ministry like today?

Paul is here carving out a new model of leadership for the church under his supervision. He is fully aware of what is happening in his society, at the same time he also knows that the power of the gospel is seen most clearly in the way it redeems human relationships. Under the gospel, people do not "use" each other and they do not dominate others. These forms of psychological oppression do not belong in the church.

GOSPEL: MATTHEW 22:34-40 (41-46); 23:1-12

Matthew 22:34-40. The question of the greatest commandment has been dealt with earlier. Here it remains only to remark that Jesus was quite capable of participating in the Torah study of his contemporaries. What is it that the law requires? is a question that deserves discussion wherever people take life and its covenants seriously, realize that priorities have to be set, and decisions made. They also realize that life cannot be carried out by clichés. At the edge of all intellectual growth stands the question, "What do you think?" This is still fundamental for kingdom existence. (For more on these verses, see the Twenty-Second Sunday after Pentecost.)

Matthew 23:1-12. One of the most difficult questions in Scripture is whether Jesus really spoke like this. There are two issues: Is Jesus' attitude towards the Pharisees reflected here, and if so, how does it square with his

teaching to love one's enemies? How did Matthew's community understand Jesus on the role of teachers in their community?

This material is a reflection of the struggle going on after 70 C.E.
between the synagogue and the church in Galilee. With the temple gone,
that competition increased, because Christians were intent upon a self-
definition distinct from Judaism. Jews in Galilee, under Rome's effective
leadership, were also on the way to resurrecting Judaism after the fall of
the temple. Hardly a shred of political power remained, few institutions
still stood, so the definition of community was essential.

Matthew's readers are told that the credentials of the scribes and Pharisees are impeccable: "They sit in the chair of Moses. Do what they tell
you and listen to what they say." It is hard to believe that this is addressed
to Christians who are no longer Jews! But perhaps it is a case of Jesus
showing his conservative side; of Jesus affirming the institution before
criticizing its abuse. At any rate, he describes the false ways (vv. 1-7)
before depicting the true way (vv. 8-12).

To be sure, there follows a scathing indictment of the devotion paid to
attracting attention, taking places of honor, seeking fawning greetings and
above all having people call them "rabbi." Every minister, living in whatever village, town, or city in North America, is well acquainted with the
routine. Moreover, we can add housing allowances, tax concessions, free
golf on Mondays, clergy discounts, free club memberships, and so on. And
who would ever think of calling us anything but "Father," or the Protestant
equivalent, "Reverend"? Who of us is prepared to abide by the rule of
Jesus so clearly stated here?

The condemnation Matthew's community placed on being called rabbi
is very clear. In contrast to the scribes and the Pharisees who love to be
called rabbi, Jesus says, "Don't you ever allow yourself to be called rabbi.
For one is your teacher and you are all equal brothers and sisters." Titles
have a way of separating us from each other. Besides, they obscure the fact
that Jesus is our only teacher. The restriction is strengthened with two further commands: No one is to be called father, for God is our Father (v. 9);
no one is to be called leader, for one is your leader, the Christ (v. 10).

Adolf Schlatter, one of the greatest commentators to live in this century,
describes the "repudiation of all religious grandeur as the constitution of
the new Church." Jesus forbids his disciples to be given titles; the work
they can do, but the honor of titles belongs only to Jesus.

While scholars admit that these words of Jesus have been expanded by
the community to fit their situation, they also recognize that none of Jesus'
words are more clear in their restriction of titles and none more widely dis-
regarded. At the same time, this flagrant violation of the rule of the gospel

has not been put to noble service. Most often it has strengthened the bonds of the hierarchy or the teachers of the church. It has violated the equality basic to the community Christ formed.

John P. Meier invites his own Catholic community "to reflect on whether these inspired words call it to forsake the ecclesiastical titles which have proliferated in its midst, especially since one of its most common titles, 'Father,' is specifically forbidden to religious leaders" (*Matthew,* New Testament Message Series [Collegeville, Minn.: Liturgical Press, 1980]).

All Christians have considerable work to do in this area, for what Jesus aims at here is not achieved simply by abolishing titles. Even Paul seems not to have heard of this teaching, for he built churches in which equality was practiced, but he did not hesitate to claim the role of "father" (1 Cor. 4:15; Gal. 4:19; Philemon 10), although no one addressed him with that title. In the emotional farewell between Elisha and Elijah, the former cries, "My father, my father" (2 Kings 2:12). Still, most likely, neither Elijah nor Paul were generally addressed as "father."

A man came to Jesus one day, addressing him as "good master"; Jesus rebuked the man by reminding him that only one, namely God, is good (Matt. 19:16-30; Mark 10:17-31; Luke 18:18-30). The teaching ministry of Jesus and of his followers deserves to be respected. At the same time, it is performance that counts, not degrees hanging on a wall or titles trailing after one's name on the marquee outside the church building. Precisely, when people request using titles for us, we should remind them of Jesus' teaching of equality and how easy it is to lose the true nature of the church when we allow them to pay us this "compliment."

What Matthew has handed down to us here about Jesus' teaching has its first application in his own community and its power struggles. At the same time, in the light of the abuse of power and the way that abuse is often fostered by titles like professor, reverend, father, and so forth, we do well to heed the warnings of Jesus.

As far as we can see, Paul never invoked his title as apostle to strengthen his authority. Instead, he said, "I have written you rather boldly in part to refresh your memories based on the grace given me by God" (Rom. 15:15-16). Like Paul, we all serve, authorized by the grace we have received from God, and it is that grace which we are to hand on, not knowledge or power or influence. Whatever titles are imposed on us by people, our only authority is one of grace. That is the calling which demands more than we can ever offer it, but it also has a rich potential for joy and fulfilment in service to others.

A modern trend in business leadership is called "servant leadership." The emphasis is not on status but on mutual empowerment. The prototype is a network in which each link is important and each of us seeks to strengthen the other. Women, like Sally Helgesen in the business world, have been leaders in articulating this model of leadership. Does this sound like the church? Unfortunately, most churches are modeled after the Roman military with its strict hierarchical structure and definitions of rank and duties. More than anything, we love our titles.

We had best apply these verses first to ourselves before we think of Pharisees or others who seek to follow God's ways. Whatever you make of Jesus' sharp criticism here, think of him as an insider, as a loyal Jew himself, and, above all, that he did not violate his own command to love his enemies. The Second Vatican Council got it right: "Respect and love ought to be extended also to those who think or act differently than we do in social, political, and religious matters, too. In fact, the more deeply we come to understand their ways of thinking through such courtesy and love, the more easily will we be able to enter into dialogue with them" (p. 28).

Twenty-Fourth Sunday after Pentecost
Thirty-First Sunday in Ordinary Time
Proper 27

Lectionary	First Lesson	Psalm	Second Lesson	Gospel
Revised Common	Wis. 6:12-16 or Amos 5:18-24	Psalm 70 or Wis. 6:17-20	I Thess. 4:13-18	Matt. 25:1-13
Episcopal (BCP)	Amos 5:18-24	Psalm 70	I Thess. 4:13-18	Matt. 25:1-13
Roman Catholic	Mal. 1:14b—2:2b, 8-10	Ps. 34:2-3, 17-19, 23	I Thess. 2:7b-9, 13	Matt. 23:1-12
Lutheran (LBW)	Amos 5:18-24	Ps. 63:1-8	I Thess. 4:13-14 (15-18)	Matt. 25:1-13

HERMENEUTICAL REFLECTIONS

The lections for this Sunday are eschatological in tone, if not also in content. Amos and Malachi remind us of the inevitability of divine retribution for those who ignore justice and mercy. Paul outlines the sequence of end-events (the resurrection of Jesus, the return of Christ, the resurrection of the dead believers, and the transformation of the believers still living). Matthew speaks of alertness and watchfulness.

Notice in these lections the strong blending of the ideas of justice and mercy. Amos thunders about justice rolling down like waters; Malachi pronounces judgment on a corrupt priesthood; Paul speaks about hope and encouragement; and Matthew presents a parable that leaves questions of justice in an enigma.

The times we live in are short on forgiveness. Confrontation, accusations, and publicity are the order of the day. The sparks of hatred are easily ignited and spread like a prairie fire. There is, sad to say, a strong movement to discredit forgiveness and to take vengeance into one's own hands. It is not the way of Jesus and if the church is to be the church, it will have to disown this rejection of forgiveness. For to be the church means not only to declare that God is a forgiving God, but also to live out that forgiveness in community. The courage to heal and the courage to be healed in the body of Christ rest on a continuing process of being forgiven our sins by God even as we forgive others their sins against us.

FIRST LESSON: WISDOM 6:12-16; AMOS 5:18-24; MALACHI 1:14B—2:2B, 8-10

Wisdom 6:12-16. The book of Wisdom, also called the Wisdom of Solomon, was written in Greek by a Jew who had been exposed to Greek influences. Since he quotes the Septuagint (the Greek Old Testament trans-lated around 200 B.C.E.), he must have written between the years 200 b.c.e. and 50 C.E. He writes an elegant Greek and shows a strong devotion to Judaism for he is devoted to the God of the Fathers (9:1) and expresses his pride in belonging to the "holy people" and a "blameless race" (10:15). Most likely he lived in Alexandria and probably wrote about fifty years before the birth of Jesus.

The title indicates the theme of the book: wisdom personified (cf. Proverbs 8; Sirach 24), which is highly praised throughout the book. Although the author is neither a philosopher nor a theologian, as a sage he/she commends wisdom. Wisdom is traditionally defined as born of God, as the central component of all virtue, and obtained by prayer. Did not Solomon, when invited to ask whatever he wanted of God in the inau-guration of his reign, ask for wisdom? The author advances beyond this in adding more recent contemporary knowledge to wisdom and also address-es the problem of retribution.

The book has been deeply appreciated by many Christians and the litur-gy has made free use of it. Its use of historical materials is an excellent example of midrash, an exegetical method later associated with the rabbis. The author's debt to the Greeks is evident in the use of the four cardinal virtues: self-control, courage, justice, and prudence (8:7).

The text describes the accessibility of wisdom. She is not elitist. She does not inhabit the mystery cults or those who have rigorous initiation rites. The only requirement is to love her and she is readily seen. She even anticipates desire for her and makes herself available to those who long for her. The one who merely thinks about her already has full-grown understanding and to be alert for her means that all anxiety flees. But wisdom does not merely sit at the gate and make herself available. She also goes in search of those worthy of her and draws them into her lov-ing discipline.

At this stage in Jewish history, wisdom is seen as an embodied divine attribute—she is not a separate deity but a personified form through which God reveals the divine nature. Later this would change, especially in cer-tain forms of Gnosticism.

Amos 5:18-24. How very different the thundering of the fig picker, cat-tleman, or shepherd from Tekoa sounds! Tekoa is a village beneath the shadow of Herodium; today it is a thriving settlement built on appropriated Arab land. Amos, one of the earliest prophets, set the standards for many others to come. Vividly he describes in today's text what will happen to the people who unctuously declare their eagerness to see the day of the Lord arrive. Their longing for that date will mean the opposite of what they expect and every attempt to escape will be met with a greater evil. In the end it will be gloom, "without a single ray of light" (v. 20). As a dweller of Judah in the south, he preached mainly in the north. Israel showed no remorse and so Amos became a prophet of doom.

The strongest prophetic language declares God's hatred for feasts and offerings: "Stop your sacrifices for I refuse even to look at your sacrifices of fattened calves" (v. 22). Sharp as this sounds, it is likely not to be taken as a rejection of the cultus as such but an attempt to restore perspective. Let them not hide behind the sacrifices but let justice flow like water and integrity like an unfailing stream.

Both Isaiah and Amos like to use the imagery of the rolling stream in their descriptions of justice and peace. This is easily understood. For Martin Luther King, Jr., it may have been a reminder of the mighty Mississippi, but for Amos it most likely had parallels to the river Jordan, virtually the only river known to him. To Isaiah it could have meant the Nile or the Euphrates. At any rate, without the river, the land dies. And so the people of God, devoid as they are of justice, in their time of prosperity were denounced for their feasts, for they could not cover up their crime with religiosity. What happens at worship must fit with what happens at the market and in the home.

"Bring me no more of your bull" writes one translator and it is an apt description of God's response to such a diversion of true religion into ceremony and cant.

Malachi 1:14b—2:2b, 8-10. If Amos found social injustice in the high echelons of power in the Northern Kingdom, Malachi found laxness, defilement, and factionalism among the ruling priests and the people of Jerusalem in the rebuilt temple in the early Persian period, the first part of the fifth century B.C.E.

The prophet denounces degeneration and laxity: the people are reneging on their tithes; they are practicing intermarriage; the unfortunate are being oppressed. The priestly leaders, in particular, are culpable, because they have fought among themselves (probably a feud between the Zadokites and the levitical priesthood) and, what is worse, have "caused many to stumble" (2:8); they are guilty of malfeasance in office.

Malachi appeals to the word and the character of God: God is a great King, whose name "is referenced among the nations" (1:14). God is the father of all sides in the community, the creator of all. How, then, can there be oppression of one by another, strife and contention and disobedience to the ritual and moral demands of the law?

The lesson ends with a plea that is appropriate for all communities, including Christian congregations: "Why then are we faithless to one another, profaning the covenant of our ancestors?" (2:10). Divisiveness and factionalism in our religious communities are to be taken seriously, and the religious leaders are to tend to the well-being of those in their care.

SECOND LESSON: I THESSALONIANS 4:13-18

In this material, written in the early fifties c.e., we encounter probably the earliest Christian apocalyptic writing. For the first time, Paul has brought the gospel to the Western Hemisphere and has proclaimed what is typical in Jewish thought, namely the Day of the Lord. The use of apocalyptic language and images brought forward a serious misunderstanding on the part of the Thessalonians, who were, no doubt, unacquainted with this style of discourse.

1 Thessalonians 4:1—5:11 is an attempt to encourage the members of that struggling congregation (4:18; 5:11), to give them a resource for building up each other, as indeed they are already doing. No category is more basic to Paul's work with congregations than the idea of "building each other up." This is central to Pauline thought about Christian community and the essential element in all that he did. J. Paul Sampley has shown that Paul is committed to the idea of the oneness of the church. It was part of the Roman legal system that unanimity in a group was the charter of their existence. Once they lost unanimity, the society dissolved. For Paul, certainly, the loss of unanimity was a denial of the presence of Christ. To the Corinthians, he asks impatiently, "Is Christ divided?" (1 Cor. 1:13).

The apocalyptic language here also has been transformed. In contrast to much previous apocalyptic material, the dominant mood for this material is the affirmation of hope. We belong, Paul affirms, to those who are children of the day, not children of the night. Destruction cannot hurt us. To be sure, the Lord, he believes, will return and will bring back to life those who have died. It will come by surprise. Especially those who believe the cry that there is "peace and security" will be surprised. Destruction will come upon them with labor pains like that of a pregnant woman.

Therefore, as in Mark 13 and in most apocalyptic writings, including above all the book of Revelation, the invitation is one to wakefulness. To be asleep when Christ returns is to miss a very great opportunity, and to be sober is a hallmark of the children of light. This term "children of light" is exactly what the people of the sect of Qumran called themselves. They too had a strong apocalyptic dimension, which meant simply that they knew that the present state of the world could not endure. God could not forever tolerate human disobedience; some, however, were destined for salvation.

Paul democratizes the military images of Isaiah (59:16-18; 63:9) and also of the book of Wisdom (18:14-25). Here it is the community that puts on as armor, faith and love, and as helmet, the hope of salvation. Faith, hope, and love, that energizing triad Paul affirmed so strongly in 1 Corinthians 13, 1 Thessalonians 1:1-4, and elsewhere, becomes here a weapon with which the Christian prepares for the final battle. The main point, however, that Paul makes is the invitation to live with Christ: whether day or night, whether awake or asleep, they are to encourage each other with the invitation to live with Christ (1 Thess. 5:10). No category in Paul's own theology was more central to his existence than to be in Christ. He affirmed it here in the first epistle he wrote, with characteristic boldness, even though here he uses the term "with Christ" equally often.

(For 1 Thess. 2:7b-9, 13, see the Twenty-third Sunday after Pentecost.)

GOSPEL: MATTHEW 25:1-13

Two parables in Matthew 25 stress the importance of responsible living under the kingship of Christ. The first has to do with the ten bridesmaids, five of whom are foolish and five are wise. Half of them prepared for the happy event, and the other five did not. When the bridegroom came, the foolish felt that they should be able to get the help of the wise, but no such help was forthcoming. They missed the coming of the bridegroom, and the admonition of the parable and its application is to "keep awake for you know neither the day nor the hour."

It is remarkable how often in the Gospels great opportunities are missed simply by drowsiness. One thinks of the sleepy disciples at the Transfiguration, in "deep sleep" (Luke 9:32), and the same affliction at the time Jesus was in the Garden of Gethsemane. Jesus, somewhat impatiently, asks his disciples whether they are not able to stay awake with him, at least for a brief period of time (Mark 14:32-42; Matt. 26:36-46; Luke 22:39-46).

In the spiritual life, as in all life, alertness is a precondition to survival. It has been pointed out that the wise virgins could not help the foolish ones, even if they had wanted to, for in this parable bordering on allegory, the good works cannot be automatically transferred to others. There is nothing automatic about being in the kingdom, or being received by the bridegroom when he comes.

The image of the bride is found at a number of points in Scripture. We notice it in Hosea (see the Twenty-Fifth Sunday after Pentecost), but it is most dominant in the book of Canticles. There, the bridegroom/bride relationship, described in beautiful physical terms, became for both the Jews, and later, for Christians, a model of the relationship between the individual soul and its Creator or the people of God and its Lord.

HOMILETICAL REFLECTIONS

An Israeli journalist recently wrote a column in which he suggested the world learn from Israel how to deal with terrorist attacks. Among other things he said about revenge: "If denial is the great buffer of the human psyche in a terror-impacted land, another oft-maligned characteristic, revenge, is the greatest solace. Turning your cheek is poor counter-terror strategy. Getting back at your tormentors—an eye for an eye—may have only limited value in deterring true believers from further acts of terrorism. But it provides the psychological balm that permits a society beset by terror to feel that it retains a measure of control" (A. Rabinovich, *International Herald Tribune*, 8 May 1995).

In the wake of the World Trade Center bombing and the Oklahoma City tragedy those comments strike a responsive chord. Let it only be said that it runs directly against the central message of the whole Bible. That message affirms that the most important way we have of "getting even" is to trust that God is still in control and that vengeance can safely be left in divine hands. Surely that is the healthiest response for individuals. Nations might do better to get at the roots of such violence and provide an opportunity for the disadvantaged to find their life's goal in more constructive things.

The cycle of abuse and violence must be stopped. Let it end with us as we learn to die with Christ and learn to absorb the hatred of others and transform it into the love of God. Jesus took upon himself enormous abuse and ultimately transformed it into a triumph over injustice, hatred, and evil. In our day, many people continue to find that way not only to be one of integrity but also one that brings with it wholeness of a quite different order than to retread the old forms of revenge.

Young Kim's mother, dying as a result of Khmer Rouge soldiers' action, said to him, "Remember, your father's and mother's blood. It is calling out in revenge for you." Interviewed by Roger Rosenblatt for his book *Children of War* (New York: Doubleday, 1992), Kim declared he was going to take revenge, but said "to me revenge means that I must make the most of my life." Another ten-year-old boy, also committed to revenge, defined it this way: "Revenge is to make a bad person better than before." Although spoken by a Buddhist, surely these words capture what is at the heart of Jewish, Christian, and Muslim teaching on retaliation. It waits only to be transformed into life.

Twenty-Fifth Sunday after Pentecost
Thirty-Second Sunday in Ordinary Time
Proper 28

Lectionary	First Lesson	Psalm	Second Lesson	Gospel
Revised Common	Zeph. 1:7, 12-18	Ps. 90:1-8 (9-11), 12	I Thess. 5:1-11	Matt. 25:14-30
Episcopal (BCP)	Zeph. 1:7, 12-18	Psalm 90 *or* 90:1-8, 12	I Thess. 5:1-10	Matt. 25:14-15, 19-29
Roman Catholic	Wis. 6:12-16	Ps. 63:2-8	I Thess. 4:13-18 *or* 4:13-14	Matt. 25:1-13
Lutheran (LBW)	Hosea 11:1-4, 8-9	Ps. 90:12-17	I Thess. 5:1-11	Matt. 25:14-30

FIRST LESSON: WISDOM 6:12-16; HOSEA 11:1-4, 8-9; ZEPHANIAH 1:7, 12-18

Wisdom 6:12-16. The book of Wisdom is a didactic exhortation, a literary form well known in Greek literature. It represents a blend of philosophy and rhetoric and is a practical appeal to one's learning and the impact that learning should have on one's ethical behavior.

In this section, the author praises the accessibility of wisdom. Wisdom is not reserved only for the few, but easily discovered by those who love her and found by those who seek her. It will not be difficult finding her, for she sits in a public place and, to concentrate on wisdom, to be vigilant for her, results in freedom from care. She goes about looking for those worthy of her and graciously appears to those while they are still on the path and comes out to meet them in every single thought. Wisdom is highly praised. Her radiance and her unfading quality make her worthy of pursuit. An encounter with her is available to everybody. (For more on these verses, see the Twenty-Fourth Sunday after Pentecost.)

Zephaniah 1:7, 12-18. This literature is classic apocalyptic. It unveils a future time when those who do not expect God to do anything will have a rude awakening. They rest complacently evaluating their tea leaves, or looking at the bottom of their wine glasses. They are sure that God can do neither good nor harm, but will find their wealth plundered and their houses laid to waste.

This is a classic description of the coming of the "great day of the Lord"; an affirmation and hope found in many apocalyptic writers that the day is very near. In classical prophetic and apocalyptic terms, it is described as a day of wrath, a day of distress and anguish, of darkness and gloom. It is a time of great tribulation but the people who have sinned against the Lord must have their day of reckoning. Their end is described in bloody terms. The day of the Lord's wrath and the fire of God's passion will consume the whole earth; a full and terrible end will be made of all the inhabitants of the earth.

This type of language flourishes today among certain sects, but the institutional church has not found it to be conducive to its chosen style of life. At the same time, underneath it, if we listen carefully, we can hear the cry for justice and for an affirmation of the sovereignty of God in a world where such sovereignty is seldom seen and even less often acknowledged.

These writers call us to silence in the midst of the difficulties of life (1:7). Instead of more action, let alone more shouting, the apocalyptic writer invites us to be silent and to wait for the Lord.

One recalls the cry of the martyrs' blood in Rev. 6:9-11, which also results in an admonition to wait a little longer. This is perhaps the most difficult instruction given to us in the whole Bible, for we are so confident that God wants us to act that we find it extremely hard to be silent. Yet, it may well be that it is only when we are silent that God can do a work of grace among us. "Wait for the Lord" is the repeated invitation of the Psalms and we find that exceedingly difficult, particularly for preachers or priests who are, after all, at their very best when they are articulating the glories of the divine message. Yet for us, too, the time to be silent before the Lord God is perhaps even more important. For without the silence, we have nothing to say. Is it possible that God can only speak when we are silent? And why were the ears of the ancient priests in the Israelite temple anointed, if not to stress that God's servant must listen before speaking?

Hosea 11:1-4, 8-9. It is ironical that this early statement of Yahweh's love for God's people comes to us through the acted parable of a failed marriage. Chapter 11 is a particularly strong and tender description of God's love for the people described through the events that led God to call Israel as a child from Egypt. Love here triumphs over whatever betrayal there may have been. The covenant relationship continues. God, as indeed Hosea, did not stop calling for the beloved. The covenant is confirmed by recalling the actions of the past, when God picked Israel up and the arms of God cradled her. They were unaware of the healing influence God had upon them or the bonds of love with which God drew them. At the same time, this book shows the passion of God and the strong (we may almost say erotic) dimensions of love that are expressed toward Israel.

Hosea is only the first to use the image of marriage between God and Israel. In graphic and tasteless detail, it is also used in Ezekiel 16 and 23 and becomes a favorite topic for the later writers. Even the document found at Qumran, called sometimes the "Wiles of the Wicked Woman," is not to be seen as a generic chauvinist document trying to prove the superiority of males. That genre of literature, well-known among the ancients, reached its nadir, about the time the book of Genesis was written, in the poem of Simonides called "Why God Created Women." Marriage is an apt figure of speech for the relation of God to the people, for both in our capacity to *make* covenants with each other and our tendency to *break* covenants, the marriage relationship closely resembles our union with God.

The image of God as parent is also a precious one. Those who object that God should always be referred to in male terms, such as "father," should be reminded that Isaiah is quite comfortable using such female metaphors as "birthing" ("I formed you in my womb," 44:2).

Mayer Gruber has pointed out that there are at least four verses in Second Isaiah (42:14; 45:10; 49:15; 66:13), one verse in each of its principal divisions, where the prophet explicitly depicts the Lord as a mother. The writer is alone among biblical writers in doing that, for in the rest of Hebrew Scripture the Lord is explicitly depicted only as a father.

It is possible that by engaging in gender-matched, synonymous parallelism and making it clear that God is above gender, the author was trying to stem the tide of Israelite women leaving their faith. There are feminine attributes to God as well as masculine ones. Modern critics of feminism and opponents to inclusive language should note this technique and certainly Christians should note that more inclusive language pertaining to God is quite frequent in the writings of the early Christians.

Whatever the reason for that among the prophets, the writers of the earliest Christian documents were obviously influenced by the inclusiveness of Jesus. It was, after all, one of the hallmarks of his ministry that women traveled with him—a practice no modern theologian, evangelist, or church official could adopt without scandal. Even the famous orchestra conductor Antol Dorati, when asked why he would not hire women for his orchestra, replied that groups could not travel with women without problems. Obviously, he had never allowed himself to think of the problems men cause when they travel in groups!

The cry, "How can I hand you over, how can I give you up?" is answered by the reflection that the heart recoils within God, the compassion grows warm and tender, and fear and anger will not be executed. The reason for this is that it is contrary to the nature of God. God's nature is not like that of a mortal, and the promise, "I will not come in wrath," is surely one of the clearest windows on the nature of God. It is the most moving description of God's relationship of love toward the people of God found anywhere in the Holy Scripture. It is also noteworthy that the theme of God's visitation, so central to apocalyptic thought becomes, especially in Luke, shorthand for God visiting us in the person of Christ.

SECOND LESSON: I THESSALONIANS 5:1-11

In this passage, Paul tries to calm the eschatological anxiety of his converts in Thessalonica. Paul's missionary preaching in synagogues and towns of Asia Minor and Greece no doubt included an emphasis on the "last things." He understood Jesus' resurrection as the "first fruits" of the final resurrection (1 Cor. 15:20). At times, he left the impression that the ultimate End was near; the return of Christ, the resurrection of the dead believers, and the transformation of believers still living would occur "like a thief in the night" (1 Thess. 5:2), without warning. These thoughts are clear in the verses (4:13-18) that immediately precede the second lesson for this week. Amos's "Day of the Lord" is, for Paul, the return of Christ and the events that accompany it (5:2).

But when would this take place? At least some believers in Thessalonica became fearful and wondered whether a radical change in life-style was in order. Should they continue their daily work (1 Thess. 4:11; 2 Thess. 3:11)? Were customary moral values to be ignored? Should they plan for their earthly future?

Paul's response to the eschatological anxiety of the Thessalonians is reasonable, clear, and worthy of emulation. They are neither to give themselves to moral abandon (vv. 6-7) nor to hysterics (v. 11). Instead they are to pay attention to the three basic Christian virtues: faith, hope, and love: "Put on the breastplate of faith and love, and for a helmet the hope of salvation" (v. 8).

No one had a more passionate faith in Christ than Paul. His turn to Christ had involved radical change—social, personal, convictional, and other. But when his converts tended toward extremism he always called them back to the center: "Our Lord Jesus Christ . . . died for us, so that whether we are awake [alive] or asleep [having died] we may live with him" (vv. 9-10). By cultivating faith, hope, and love in their day-to-day lives, they will "encourage one another and build up each other" (v. 11).

Extremism, fanaticism, and polarization are becoming ever more attractive to persons and groups in our time. As members of the body of Christ we would do well to confront false ideology, and the kind of turning inward that makes us oblivious to the needs of our neighbor. Most especially, Paul advises us to encourage one another and to fasten our attention on what is most important: a healthy faith, a lively hope, and active love.

(For 1 Thess. 4:13-18, see the Twenty-Fourth Sunday after Pentecost.)

GOSPEL: MATTHEW 25:14-30

The second parable in Matthew 25, that of the talents has a similar point to the parable of the ten bridesmaids, found in last week's lectionary readings—namely, to be vigilant and to use the time to good advantage and not to assume that a lethargical approach will do. The faithful servant is one who has "multiplied" the talents; the same word that is used here means to win over people into the community (compare Matthew 18:15). The servant who does not put his talent to use and allow it to grow is harshly condemned to outer darkness. He is considered worthless because he has not only misjudged the nature of the master, but has simply been unwilling to take any kind of risk.

Those who take the risk of letting what they have grow are rewarded and invited to enter into the joy of their Master. And joy is a characteristic note in the New Testament; it is one of the three elements that constitute the kingdom of God, as Paul defines it in Romans 14:16. Christians took from Judaism this affirmation of joy as central to the covenant. The epistle of Barnabas some decades later called the Christians "children of joy."

We will find it much easier to live with and even to live from apocalyptic literature if we observe that it is one of the richest fruits of Judaism, virtually not found at all outside of Judaism in the ancient world. Contemporary Judaism does not have much to say about this genre of literature and it is sometimes assumed that after Christianity left the fold, Judaism did not imitate the Christian appropriation of this part of their heritage.

At any rate, apocalypticism is a product of the struggle between king and prophet, mainly in the postexilic period. Sometimes we are told that it is a literature born of despair but that is incorrect, it is the literature of hope. The Greeks had no use for hope, calling it "the bread of exiles," or the lie with which one nudged the people forward to fight in a losing battle. Not so the Hebrews.

The firm faith of the Hebrews that God would redeem them and that a time would come when God's sovereignty would be established, even though there was no evidence of that at the moment, is what kindled this literature. Hope is central to both the Jewish and the Christian faith, as well as to all life. Without hope, we literally perish. For hope is not merely the compulsion to repeat, so aptly illustrated in Robert Burns' poem about the spider that keeps trying to scale the wall until it succeeds. Hope is the indomitable conviction that life is worth living and that a God of love deigned to make a covenant with us and will not play us false. God cannot be untrue to Godself.

The theme of this literature is also joy. How significant that the phrase "entering into the joy of the Lord" becomes the description of the reward for those who take risks in life. How fundamental is the story of Abraham who answered the call, left Haran, and marched off into a country for which there were no maps. Faith can be a leap into the unknown even as it can be (and often is) a solid plodding on when there is only darkness and drudgery and pain and suffering. But the faith of the Bible fundamentally celebrates God's grace and that celebration is characterized by joy.

Joy is not found at cocktail parties where people talk past each other. It is not found in the emptiness of the theatrics of the stadium even when it is sold right out and the game is tightly and masterfully played. Curiously, joy is not even found in the comedian's efforts. Entertainers, who are most successful in getting others to laugh, are themselves often prone to depression. Finally, it is must be said that joy cannot be created by ritual in a church service.

The Gospel invites us to shift from John the Baptist, an austere herald of punishment and vengeance, to Jesus, announced as the bridegroom who has come to celebrate a wedding. The musical Godspell caught that mood even as it caught the changes that took place among the people who followed Jesus.

Pierre van Passen, in his book *Earth Could be Fair*, depicts the spontaneity of an organist whose patience wore out one Sunday when his pastor once more had found some vinegar in a biblical text. Casting aside his music, he played instead Handel's "Hallelujah" chorus with all the volume his organ could produce. The people got the point. The church that makes the joy of the Lord its strength will prosper and the servants of the church who communicate that joy through all they do will feel at home when they enter into the joy of the Lord at the end of the race and join their voice to the choruses magnifying the name of the Lord.

Last Sunday after Pentecost
Christ the King
Proper 29

Lectionary	First Lesson	Psalm	Second Lesson	Gospel
Revised Common	Ezek. 34:11-16, 20-24	Ps. 95:1-7a	Eph. 1:15-23	Matt. 25:31-46
Episcopal (BCP)	Ezek. 34:11-17	Ps. 95:1-7	I Cor. 15:20-28	Matt. 25:31-46
Roman Catholic	Ezek. 34:11-12, 15-17	Ps. 23:1-6	I Cor. 15:20-26, 28	Matt. 25:31-46
Lutheran (LBW)	Ezek. 34:11-16, 23-24	Ps. 95:1-7a	I Cor. 15:20-28	Matt. 25:31-46

FIRST LESSON: EZEKIEL 34:11-17, 20-24

One of the favorite images of the God of Israel is that of the shepherd. In the land, shepherds were a familiar sight. We notice that the pursuing, aggressive, proactive nature of God is expressed in the searching that God does for the sheep. They will be sought out.

The Scripture depicts also different kinds of sheep. The shepherd is able not only to take the sheep to good pastures, but also to sort out these different kinds of sheep. Some have strayed, some are weary and crippled; there are rams and he-goats.

As in Psalm 23, so here Ezekiel portrays Yahweh as one who will take the sheep to good grazing land and they shall feed on rich pasture. Sheep who foul the water as they feed in it will be punished (vv. 17-19), and those who have aggressively pushed each other with flank and shoulder and butted at all of the weak animals with their horns will be scattered. The promise is that the flock will be saved. The strong will be destroyed (v. 16), for the flock will be fed in justice. It will no longer be ravished and eventually David will be the true shepherd of the sheep.

The image of the shepherd as leader of a people is very common in the Near East and is often applied to a king. How one interprets that image in today's urban society when God is the subject is not an easy problem to solve. Perhaps the superintendent of an apartment complex, the police who keep traffic flowing and a semblance of order in our society, perhaps those who arrange for tax rebates and a just administration of our laws in other ways, are the closest parallel. In any case, what Ezekiel promises in this discourse is the establishment of a "covenant of peace" (34:25) when wild animals will be banished from the land and people will be able to live in the wild and sleep in the woods securely.

This blessing of secure sleep, of safety in the streets, is one that our society longs for desperately and there are few places in the world where it is a reality. Perhaps it is because people are not being fed with justice, which the true shepherd of the sheep promises above all else (v. 16). When justice becomes the daily fare, many problems of society are removed and the life of the community becomes transformed. It is an irony that an expression like "showers of blessing" (v. 26), describing a society in the covenant of peace that brings justice, security, and removal of fear and hunger, is often applied to personal salvation of the soul instead.

SECOND LESSON: I CORINTHIANS 15:20-26, 28; EPHESIANS 1:15-23

1 Corinthians 15:20-26, 28. In Paul's dealings with the Corinthians, one of the contested issues was the resurrection. As we know, when he preached in Athens on Mars Hill, the Greeks could not conceive of a resurrection (Acts 17:32). When he first preached it to the Thessalonians, they too could not comprehend it. Neither Jew nor Greek believed in a resurrection. Here, Paul integrates his view of the resurrection with his firm conviction that, eventually, Christ's resurrection, which marked the defeat of death, would come to all humankind. Consequently, he draws an analogy between the death that came to all people universally through the acts of the first person to live in history, and Christ who made all alive, he being "the first fruits" (vv. 20, 23).

Upon Christ's coming, then, Paul believes that the end will come. The end of history, as we know it, and the kingdom, which Christ inaugurated in his earthly ministry and over which he has presided over the centuries, will be handed over to God the Father. All rule, all authority, all power will be rendered ineffective. The reign of Christ, which will put all enemies under his feet, including death, the supreme enemy, will be achieved through the supreme power of God, for as Paul sees it, God had put all things under Christ's supervision and authority. The only one who will not be included in this subjection is the supreme actor, God. Paul believes firmly that everything, eventually, will be subjected to the power of God so that "God may be all and in all."

This is not an easy concept to understand and the problems it raises are not easy to resolve. The church leader Origen believed fervently in this hope and was convinced that the recapitulation accomplished by Jesus would include the salvation of all. For God to be God, eventually all would submit to the drawing power of God's love. Throughout the history of the church, there have been many people who have defended this type of universalism. They do so, not necessarily because they are unable to distinguish between good and evil, but because they have a very strong belief in the power of God's love. Moreover, they affirm these words of Paul. They believe everyone must yield eventually to the attraction of divine love.

Others believe that the human will must be respected and the enormity of sin taken seriously. Thus, the *Gospel of Bartholomew* asserted that when Jesus harrowed hell, he could not remove three people: Cain, the first to murder his brother; Herod the Great, tyrant of the first century who slaughtered the innocents; and Judas, whose despicable deed, as they saw it, against Jesus was simply unforgivable.

But Origen and others have affirmed, or at least implied, that even the devil will eventually capitulate to the love of Christ. For Paul, it was urgent that the Corinthians recognize the resurrection. He considered it inconceivable that there might be any kind of gospel without belief in the resurrection. He therefore stitches together what he has received from his predecessors with what will come in the end. All of it issues in the invitation to come to a sober and right mind and to sin no more.

One has only to read the last verses of chapter 15 to see Paul at his best. This mockery of death comes out forcefully in the Greek quote from Hosea 13:14:

> Death has been swallowed up in victory.
> Where your (*Pou sou*), victory, death?
> Where your (*Pou sou*), sting, death?

In effect, he taunts death and affirms that the victory of death is gone, the sting of death is gone, and he ends with a resounding doxology to God, giving thanks to God for the victory achieved through Jesus Christ. The ethical appeal that, therefore, the Corinthians remain steadfast, immovable, always excelling in the work of the Lord (v. 58), rests on the power shown in the resurrection.

Ephesians 1:15-23. Someone writing perhaps a generation after Paul reiterates the same theme of the hope found in Christ with the affirmation that he is all powerful and above all rule, authority, and power and dominion. In a concrete way, this is affirmed through the way in which Christ is the head of the church. Assuredly, the highest praise given to the church is found in these words that the church is the body of Christ and that, in fact, it is the fullness of him who fills all in all.

Both Colossians and Ephesians have a very high view of the church; so high, in fact, that it is difficult for us to see any relationship between that perspective and the church we all know so intimately and love so imperfectly. We do well to remember that these words, this high tribute to the church, is written by one who was first and foremost a pastor.

Paul knew well the blemishes and the spots and the wrinkles of the Corinthian church. This, however, did not shake his faith that, through the resurrection of Christ, a community had come into being for which he was profoundly thankful. This community, he believed, could be given a spirit of wisdom and revelation so that they might know what is the hope to which God called them. This specific knowledge of what God's will is for them in a concrete situation becomes the new gift of the presence of Christ and the power of the resurrection among them.

GOSPEL: MATTHEW 25:31-46

This segment is the high point of the Gospel of Matthew, and has been described as "the grand finale of the fifth discourse and of the public ministry" (Ben Viviano). It is uniquely Matthean and has no direct parallels in other Gospels. Neither a parable nor an allegory, it is instead an extensive "word-picture" describing the nature of the kingdom of God that attempts to outline the practical nature of belonging to that kingdom. This segment is addressed, in the first instance, to the disciples, so it misses the point to say, as some do, that it teaches that people can be members of the kingdom simply through good works. All the nations will be involved here, and the test of the religion, which is taught by Matthew, is very concrete.

This test has to do with service to the least of these my "brethren." Whether the word *brethren* means fellow Christians or involves a broader definition has been much debated. Certainly, in some passages in Matthew (5:22; 7:3), "brethren" refers to any human being, whereas in 18:15 it is restricted to a member of the community. So Matthew uses it in both senses.

What we have here is a description of the covenant, which is unconditional in some texts of the New Testament, but here is clearly defined by human obligation and the reality of obedience. Every judgment scene in the New Testament, some say, ends with a surprise. This is no exception, and indeed, perhaps it has the most surprising end of all. Faithfulness to God is here defined as doing very concrete deeds of love and compassion to the people who are "nobodies." They are the "least," with no rank, status, or power. Did not Jesus live this way? Should it surprise us if this is also the way in which the kingdom is described?

Success in the kingdom does not depend upon your connections but on your ability to work with and minister to the neglected ones in society. For in the neediest and the seediest you can encounter the Lord.